THE LAW AND CATHOLIC SCHOOLS:

APPROACHING THE NEW MILLENNIUM

Mary Angela Shaughnessy, SCN, Ph.D.

Department of Elementary Schools
National Catholic Educational Association
ISBN # 1-55833-104-2

Third Printing 1997

TABLE OF CONTENTS

PREFACE

During the last three years the Department of Elementary Schools of the National Catholic Educational Association encouraged Sister Mary Angela Shaughnessy to address the specific topics of grave concern for Catholic elementary school educators. The three publications that resulted addressed the legal aspects of handbooks, the legal issues associated with early childhood education, and the legal concerns related to operating an extended day program. Having addressed these specific issues, a need arose of providing Catholic elementary school teachers with an overview of the legal aspects associated with conducting a school.

The Law and Catholic Schools: Approaching the New Millennium fulfills this need. The first chapter provides an overview of law as it pertains to Catholic schools. The next three chapters explore the legal duties and responsibilities of those involved in Catholic schools. This list includes: bishops, pastors, principals, board members, teachers, students and parents of students. The final section looks at some special situations such as corporal punishment, search and seizure, negligence, child abuse and copyright laws. The book concludes with a detailed glossary.

The NCEA Department of Elementary Schools again expresses its gratitude to Sister Mary Angela Shaughnessy for providing such a helpful text which is clearly written and very readable. This fulfills the vacuum in its legal series. The department offers this report to its members with the hope that Catholic educators who are more knowledgeable in this area will be able to avoid unnecessary litigation.

Robert J. Kealey, Ed.D.   Bonnie J. Pryor
Executive Director   President
September 1991

1

Dedication

I dedicate this work, with affection and gratitude, to three former colleagues who shared the ministry of Catholic education with me and who remain true friends and excellent critics: Karen M. Juliano of Louisville, Kentucky; Patricia Seleman McDonough of Wakefield, Massachusetts; and Florence E. Walsh of Atlanta, Georgia.

Acknowledgements

To all who have aided me in my work in the area of Catholic schools and the law, I offer sincere appreciation. There are several individuals I wish to mention here. First, I wish to thank Dr. Robert Kealey, Executive Director of the NCEA Department of Elementary Schools. His encouragement of my efforts on behalf of Catholic education, and his support of this text, are deeply appreciated.

I offer thanks to my friends and colleagues at Spalding University in Louisville, Kentucky, where I am privileged to serve. Their constant support is deeply appreciated. I owe a special debt of gratitude to President Eileen Egan, SCN, Ph.D. and to Dean Mary Burns, SCN, Ph.D. of the School of Education.

Miriam Corcoran, SCN, of Louisville, Kentucky has given untiring service as proofreader and editorial advisor for this text and for all my work. I owe her much gratitude.

My deep appreciation is always with those who have shared their lives in ministry with me by participating in classes and workshops throughout the country. In particular, I thank the administrators of two programs for the preparation of Catholic school leaders: Clare Fitzgerald, SSND, of the Catholic School Leadership Program at Boston College; and Edwin McDermott, SJ, and Mary Peter Traviss, OP, of the Institute for Catholic Educational Leadership at the University of San Francisco. Their faith in my ministry is a constant source of encouragement. Finally, I thank you, the readers. May God bless you and your ministry abundantly.

Mary Angela Shaughnessy, SCN, Ph.D.
Louisville, Kentucky
September 1991

CHAPTER ONE

AN INTRODUCTION TO THE LAW

As the next millennium approaches, Catholic schools face new challenges. Perhaps no aspect of Catholic education provides greater demands than does that of the law as applied to Catholic schools. Compared with public school law, Catholic school law is a legal infant. While the law relating to public schools has been a well-developed body of law for decades, Catholic school law has emerged as its own area of the law only within the last decade.

Before the 1960s courts were reluctant to interfere in school cases, public or private. Practicing the doctrine of judicial restraint, courts decided very few cases in favor of parents, students, or teachers who sued schools. Judicial restraint was supported in the public sector by the historical doctrine of sovereign immunity. This doctrine held that a sovereign (the king in England, the state in this country) could not be sued without consent. A parallel doctrine, charitable immunity, existed which could be used as a defense in cases involving churches; because of the charitable nature of a church's work, the institution would ordinarily not be held liable for actions resulting from its negligence. These two doctrines have been abandoned, for all practical purposes, in this country. Nonetheless, charitable immunity helps to explain the mindset of many Catholic school officials: that people were not expected to sue the church and, in the unlikely event that someone did, the church would prevail. Even today some persons take refuge in the conviction that persons are not likely to sue the church.

4

Such a position is dangerous and should be abandoned.

Perhaps the most prevalent misconception concerning Catholic schools and the law is a belief that persons possess the same rights in both the public and the private sectors. Because Catholic schools are not governmental agencies, teachers and students do not possess the Constitutional protections that their public school counterparts do. The primary law governing the Catholic school is contract law.

The rights of the Catholic school to exist and of parents to send their children to Catholic schools were established by the 1925 United States Supreme Court's landmark decision in *Pierce v. Society of Sisters.* This case involved a religious community's challenge to an Oregon law that would have required all children to attend public schools. The court stated:

> The fundamental theory of liberty upon which all govern
> ments in this Union repose excludes any general power of
> the State to standardize its children by forcing them to
> accept instruction from public school teachers only. The
> child is not the mere creature of the State; those who
> nurture him and direct his destiny have the right, coupled
> with the high duty, to recognize and prepare him for
> additional obligations (p. 535).

Since the *Pierce* decision there have been no serious arguments that the right of the state to mandate compulsory education includes the right to compel attendance at state-sponsored schools. More recent issues of vouchers and tax credits raise the following question: does the state's obligation to provide an education preclude the possibility of allowing parents to choose where state funds will be spent for their children's education?

In order to understand what rights are protected in the Catholic school and what rights are not protected, it is helpful to consider the rights of public school students and teachers. Public school students and teachers are protected by the United States Constitution. The First Amendment guards the freedoms of speech, press and assembly; it further prevents government from promoting or interfering with religion (this doctrine is known as "separation of church and state.") The Fourth Amendment protects persons from unlawful search and seizure. The Fifth Amendment guarantees "due process of law" before a person can be deprived of life, liberty or property. The Fourteenth Amendment to the Constitution made the Fifth Amendment, as well as all other amendments, applicable to the states. The Civil Rights Act of 1871 (Title 42 of the United States Code, Section 1983) further protects persons whose individual Constitutional rights are denied by government authorities.

Prior to 1960, public school officials were generally protected in their actions by the doctrine of *in loco parentis*, by which school officials were considered to be acting *in the place of parents*. With the landmark Supreme Court college case of *Dixon v. Alabama*, (1961); the days of *in loco parentis* began to conclude. In *Dixon* school officials disciplined black students for taking part in a lunch counter sit in; they offered the students no notice or hearing before imposing discipline; they argued that since parents do not have to give children any due process, schools do not have to give due process since they stand "in the place of parents." The court held that students in a public institution had due process rights which had to be protected before discipline could be administered or students dismissed. The *in loco parentis* doctrine was, for all intents and purposes, abandoned.

Prior to *Dixon*, many cases brought by students had simply been dismissed by the courts because of *in loco parentis*. The courts had generally allowed school officials to discipline students and to dismiss them without even telling the students the reasons for their actions. (Cf. *Anthony v. Syracuse University* 231 N.Y.S. 435, 224 App. Div. 487 (1928); *Curry v. Lasell Seminary Co.*, 1568 Mass. 7, 1897; *Gott v. Berea College* 156 Ky. 376 (1913).)

Dixon established the procedures to be followed in student dismissals. Students had to be told what the charges against them were (*notice*); they had to be allowed a *hearing* in which they could present their side of the story; and the hearing had to occur before an *impartial tribunal*.

Dixon laid down protections for students in public colleges and universities. Prior to *Dixon,* writers had been calling for protections for students in the public and private sectors. A noted scholar of that period, Warren Seavey, wrote:

Although the formalities of a trial in a law court are not necessary, and although the exigencies of school ... life may require the suspension of one reasonably thought to have violated disciplinary rules, it seems fairly clear that a student should not have the burden of proving himself innocent. The fiduciary obligation of a school to its students not only should prevent it from seeking to hide the source of its information, but demands that it afford the student every means of rehabilitation. (p. 1410)

Seavey argued that the relationship of a university or college with its students is that of a fiduciary, one charged with acting for the benefit of those entrusted to its care. Five years after *Dixon,* Alvin Goldman (1966) argued for the acceptance of the fiduciary theory in both public and private sectors: "Certainly the private university, as a fiduciary, cannot engage in conduct bearing any taint of unreasonableness, unfairness or arbitrariness which might contrast with the public university's duties under both the fourteenth amendment and its fiduciary role" (p. 673.) Many college cases were litigated after *Dixon,* but it was nine years before the reasoning in *Dixon* would be extended to cases involving public elementary and secondary schools. *Tinker v. Des Moines Independent School District et al.* was decided in 1969. *Tinker* established the right of public school students to express themselves freely as long as such expression did not interfere with reasonable order in the school: "It can hardly be argued that either students or teachers shed their constitutional rights to freedom of speech or expression at the schoolhouse gate" (p. 506). The First and Fourteenth Amendments' protections were extended to students facing suspension and/or expulsion.

In 1974 two United States Supreme Court cases further delineated the rights laid down in *Tinker. Goss v. Lopez* required that students who were facing suspensions of ten days or less be given notice of the charges and an opportunity to refute the charges before a school official. *Wood v. Strickland* (heard the same day as *Goss)* established the fact that, although students do not have an absolute right to an education no matter what they do, they cannot be deprived of an education without procedural due process. *Wood* is perhaps best known for its finding that school officials cannot claim immunity from litigation for violation of student rights if they knew or should have known the right procedure or if they acted out of malice.

Like students, teachers in the public sector cannot be disciplined without due process of law. School districts may decide not to renew the contracts of non-tenured teachers without due process because non-tenured teachers do not have "a legitimate claim of entitlement to" renewal (*Board of Regents v. Roth* (U.S. Supreme Court, 1972). However, teachers who have a "legitimate claim of entitlement" to renewal (even in the absence of a formal tenure policy) must be given appropriate procedural due process protections (*Perry v. Sindermann* U.S. Supreme Court, 1972).

Claims to job entitlement are not absolute. In cases where a teacher alleges that the exercise of a Constitutionally protected freedom is the reason for dismissal, the teacher is not automatically entitled to reinstatement. The teacher must prove that reemployment would have followed if the Constitutionally protected activity had not occurred. (See *Pickering v. B.O.E.* 391 U.S. 563, 1968; *Givhan v. Western Line* 439 U.S. 410, 1979; and *Mt. Healthy v. Doyle* 429 U.S. 274, 1977.)

Although Catholic schools are not bound by these cases on Constitutional theories, there is a growing body of opinion that private schools can be held to similar standards of conduct on either contractual or fair play grounds. These concepts will be discussed later in this text.

State Action

Before a private school could be required to grant Constitutional protections to teachers and/or students, the substantial presence of state action must be demonstrated: the state has to be significantly involved (the court determines whether the involvement is significant) in the private school or in the contested activity.

Generally, there are four theories offered to prove state action in a private school: state funding, state control, tax-exempt status, and the public benefit or function theory. Three private school cases heard in appellate courts, two involving Catholic schools, illustrate.

In *Bright v. Isenbarger* 314 F. Supp. 1382 (1970), dismissed students alleged that state action was present because of state regulation of the school and the school's tax-exempt status. Rejecting that claim, the court stated, "[B]ecause the state of Indiana was in no way involved in the challenged actions, defendants' expulsion of plaintiffs was not state action" (p. 1395).

In a 1976 expulsion case, *Wisch v. Sanford School, Inc.*, a student maintained that the federal funding present in the private school through various governmental programs constituted state action. The court, however, disagreed:

> Plaintiff must show that there was more than "some" state action in this case; not every involvement by the state in the affairs of a private individual or organization, whether through funding or regulation, may be used as a basis for a ... Fourteenth Amendment claim. The involvement must be "substantial" (p. 1313).

Courts have been struggling with the definition of "substantial" ever since the *Wisch* decision was recorded. There is more case law to guide judges, lawyers, and litigants today, but the basic question remains, particularly in such areas as discrimination.

In the 1979 case, *Geraci v. St. Xavier High School*, a student and his father brought suit against a Catholic high school which had expelled him. The plaintiffs alleged the presence of state action. The court ruled that, even if state action were present, it would have to be so entwined with the contested activity (here, the dismissal of the student) that a symbiotic relationship could be held to exist between the state and the dismissal of the student. If no such relationship can be demonstrated, state action is not present and Constitutional protections do not apply:

> [O]ther than ascertaining that the school meets minimum standards for a high school, the state exercises no control over the school whatsoever. This is certainly not the sort of pervasive state involvement required for a finding of symbiotic state action. (p. 148)

These non-public school cases indicate that, without a finding of significant state action in a private school or an activity, the courts will not hold Catholic school administrators to the requirements of Constitutional protections. The case law should not be interpreted to mean that Catholic schools and their administrators can do anything they wish to students and the courts will not intervene because of the absence of state action. Case law is constantly being developed, and so it is difficult to lay down hard and fast rules. The fact that no case involving student discipline in the private school has ever reached the United States Supreme Court may mean that there has been no final ruling on state action in non-public schools.

The one United States Supreme Court case involving a private school teacher contesting dismissal is *Rendell-Baker v. Kohn.* This case is significant because, although the school received over 90% of its funds from the state, the Supreme Court declined to find the presence of state action significant enough to warrant Constitutional protections. Previous lower courts' decisions had indicated the difficulty of proving significant state action present in teacher dismissals in a private school.

Rendell-Baker indicates that, unless the state can somehow be shown to be involved in the contested activity (such as the dismissal of a teacher), the court will not intervene in the action. Exceptions to the *Rendell-Baker* decision would lie in the area of discrimination, a matter which will be discussed later in this text.

Laws Affecting Catholic Education in the United States

The laws affecting education in the United States today can generally be classified according to four categories: (1) Constitutional law (both state and federal); (2) statutes and regulations; (3) common law principles; and (4) contract law.

Federal Constitutional law protects individuals against the arbitrary deprivation of their Constitutional freedoms by government and government officials. Students and teachers in public schools are protected by Constitutional law since public schools are governmental agencies and the administrators of public schools are public officials. Students and teachers in private schools are not protected by federal Constitutional law because they are private agencies. (Since the focus of this work is the Catholic school, subsequent references will be to Catholic schools; it should be understood, however, that statements apply to all private schools unless indicated otherwise.)

Therefore, many actions which are prohibited in public schools are permitted in Catholic schools. For example, the First Amendment to the U.S.Constitution protects persons' rights to free speech; hence, administrators in public schools may not prohibit the expression of an unpopular political viewpoint. Since no such protection exists in the Catholic school, school administrators can restrict both student and teacher speech. As indicated above, the only situation in which a Catholic school could be required to grant Constitutional protections is if state action can be found to be so pervasive within the school that the school could be considered a state agent. To this author's knowledge, no court has found a Catholic school to be a state agent.

State constitutional law may apply to private as well as public schools. It is not unusual for a state constitution to contain a statement such as, "Anyone operating an educational institution in this state shall..." As long as whatever is required does not unfairly constrain the rights of Catholic schools and can be shown to have some legitimate educational purpose, Catholic schools can be compelled to comply with the state constitutional requirements.

Federal and state statutes and regulations govern the public school and may govern the Catholic school as well. Failure to comply with reasonable regulations can result in the imposition of sanctions. The 1983 case of *Bob Jones v. United States* illustrates this point. When Bob Jones University was found to employ racially discriminatory admissions and disciplinary policies, the Internal Revenue Service withdrew the university's tax-exempt status based on a 1970 regulation proscribing the granting of tax-exempt status to any institution which discriminated on the basis of race. Before a Catholic school will be forced to comply with a law or regulation, the state must demonstrate a *compelling interest* in the enforcement of the regulations. Black (1979) defines compelling interest as: "Term used to uphold state action in the face of attack, grounded on Equal Protection or First Amendment rights because of serious need for such state action" (p. 256).

In *Bob Jones* the government's compelling interest in racial equality was sufficient for the court to order Bob Jones University to comply with the anti-discrimination regulation or lose its tax-exempt status.

Other examples of compelling state interests in educational regulations might be curriculum or graduation requirements, teacher certification and school certification requirements. In these cases the state could very possibly prove a compelling state interest in the proper education of the public. The state cannot pass laws so restrictive that a school's existence is placed in jeopardy. The right of the Catholic school to exist was firmly established in the aforementioned *Pierce* case.

The third type of law which applies to both the public and private sector (and, indeed to all cases, whether school cases or not) is the common law. Gatti and Gatti (1983) define common law:

> Common law is the general universal law of the land. This law is not derived from state STATUTES, but is developed through court decisions over hundreds of years. Common law prevails in England and in the United States and is the controlling law unless abrogated or modified by state or

federal statutes. It should also be noted that common law may also be abrogated or modified by a constitutional amendment or decision by a higher court which adjudicates a constitutional issue. (p. 89)

Common law principles may also be considered to be derived from God's law, especially by persons in Catholic schools. Many common law principles are founded in basic morality such as that found in the Ten Commandments and in other religious writings.

Prior judicial decisions comprise an important part of common law. These decisions are often referred to as "precedents." When a lawsuit is begun, attorneys on both sides begin searching for precedents, prior cases that will support their arguments. In the United States these prior decisions can be found in courts of record from the beginnings of this country. The United States system of common law also embraces all English cases prior to the establishment of the United States. It is not unusual to find old English cases cited in modern cases.

The fourth type of law which governs both public and private school cases is contract law. Public schools are governed by contract law in some instances, especially in the area of teacher contracts. Courts can and will construe faculty handbooks as part of the contract. However, most cases involving public school teacher contracts also allege violation of Constitutionally protected interests as well, so contract law is not the only applicable law.

In the Catholic school, contract law is the predominant governing law. A contract may be defined as: "An agreement between two or more persons which creates an obligation to do or not to do a particular thing" (Black, pp. 291-92). Generally, the five basic elements of a contract are considered to be: (1) mutual assent (2) by legally competent parties for (3) consideration (4) to subject matter that is legal and (5) in a form of agreement which is legal.

Mutual assent implies that two parties entering into a contract agree to its provisions. A Catholic school agrees to provide an education to a student and, in return, parents accept that offer; a Catholic school offers a teacher a contract, and the teacher accepts. Traditional contract law teaches that a contract will only be considered a true instrument if there has been both an offer (of education or employment) by the first party and an acceptance of the same by the second party.

Consideration is what the first party agrees to do for the other party in exchange for something from the second party. The Catholic school agrees to provide educational services to a student in return for payment of tuition and adherence to school rules. The Catholic school agrees to pay the teacher a salary in return for instructional services.

Legally competent parties implies that the parties entering into the contract are lawfully qualified to make the agreement. A Catholic school is legally qualified to enter into contracts to educate students and to employ teachers. Parents are legally competent to agree to pay tuition and meet other obligations; minor students are not legally competent, and so parents or legal guardians must sign contracts on their behalf. A properly qualified teacher is a legally competent party; a person who does not possess the qualifications or skills needed to perform as an instructor would not be a legally competent party to enter into a teaching contract.

Legal subject matter assumes that the provisions of the contract are legal. An agreement that a teacher would not marry a person of another race as a condition of employment would not be legal, as such a condition would probably be construed as a violation of anti-discrimination laws and Constitutional freedoms as well.

Legal form may vary from state to state or from school system to school system. If, for example, a contract calls for witnesses, and no witnesses' signatures are found on the cotract, the document is probably not in proper legal form. If any one of the five elements of a contract is missing, the contract may be held to be null and void. Cases involving student and teacher discipline and discipline in Catholic schools often allege breach of contract:

A breach of contract occurs when a party does not perform

that which he or she was under an absolute duty to perform and the circumstances are such that his or her failure was neither justified nor excused (Gatti and Gatti, 1983, p. 124). Breach of contract can be committed by either party to the contract (the school/administrator or the teacher or student.) It is generally conceded, however, that it is futile for a school to seek to bring breach of contract charges against a teacher who wants to terminate a contract. A contract for the rendition of personal services will not be enforced; the remedy for breach of such a contract is damages, not performance of the contract. While teachers can generally break their contracts without severe consequences, schools and administrators cannot lawfully terminate a teacher's employment during a contract term without just cause. Neither can a school terminate a student's enrollment without just cause. Should a school act in such a manner, it may well be ordered to pay substantial damages to the offended party.

William D. Valente, a noted school law scholar, (1980, p. 464) offers this advice to persons in non-public schools who believe that their rights are being violated:

Thus, a teacher who is offended by private school orders that suppress speech, invade privacy, or impose disciplinary sanctions without notice or hearing must look elsewhere than to constitutional doctrines for legal relief, except in the unusual situation where the private school is considered to be engaged in official government action.

The "elsewhere" to which a person must look is generally contract law. Faculty, parents, and students must look to the provisions of contract law for protection; nonetheless, administrators are expected to proceed according to the rules and policies governing their schools. Catholic schools and their officials cannot "do anything they want" and escape penalties. Thus, everyone involved in the Catholic school should understand the provisions of the contracts which govern relationships among all parties concerned.

CHAPTER TWO

BISHOPS, PASTORS, PRINCIPALS, AND BOARDS: RIGHTS AND RESPONSIBILITIES

The existence of, and the roles of all parties involved in, Catholic schools are governed by canon law, the law of the Catholic Church. Civil law recognizes the right of religious organizations to govern themselves. This right, as the chapter on teacher rights and responsibilities will indicate, is not absolute. Civil courts will not allow religious institutions to evade legal responsibilities by invoking church law. Within the wide parameter imposed by civil law, though, churches have significant autonomy.

Canon law controls both the existence and continuance of Catholic institutions. A school can call itself Catholic only with the approval of the bishop. All Catholic schools are subject to the bishop in matters of faith and morals and in all other matters prescribed by the Code of Canon Law.

The bishop has final responsibility for all laws in his diocese. He may, and probably does, delegate much of his power to other parties and bodies in the diocese, such as the superintendent, the vicar, diocesan boards, and similar bodies. Although he may delegate power, he can never delegate responsibility. Like the civil theory of *respondeat superior* (the superior must answer for the actions of subordinates) the bishop must answer in canon law for the actions of his designates.

The canon law equivalent of the civil corporation is the juridic person, an individual legal entity recognized by the Church. Schools may be either separate juridic persons or part of the juridic person of a larger entity such as a parish or religious congregation.

Although a thorough consideration of Canon Law is beyond the scope of this work, it may be helpful to examine briefly the four types of Catholic schools found in this country today.

The first type is the parish elementary or high school that operates as part of a parish governed by a pastor who is the ultimate authority in that parish, subject only to the bishop. It is important for everyone associated with the school to understand that the governance of it is not a democracy. As the bishop has final responsibility for the diocese, the pastor has final responsibility for the parish, limited only by the bishop's right to review.

Today the pastor shares his decision-making with many persons in the parish. He may well operate in a spirit of collegiality. He stands alone in a very real sense under canon law, however, in his ultimate responsibility for the decisions that guide the life of his parish and hence, of the parish school.

A second type of school is the regional school, a kind of hybrid of the parish and diocesan school. It is not uncommon to see a number of parish schools consolidating and becoming regional schools. Governance structures may take different forms in regional schools. In some, one pastor has the final responsibility; others implement a model of shared decision-making among the pastors of the parishes supporting the school.

A third type of school, the diocesan school, has been associated with secondary education. In recent years dioceses have begun to sponsor regional elementary schools. Diocesan schools are established, or at least approved, by the bishop and are directly under his authority or that of his delegate, e.g., the superintendent of schools. Different government structures are possible. Some are governed by boards with the pastors of all the schools sitting on the boards and all board actions subject to the approval of those pastors; others are governed by boards subject to the final authority of one pastor designated as the one responsible for the school. Other diocesan schools have been established without any association with a given parish or parishes; these schools may be governed by a board which is under the direct jurisdiction of the bishop. The question of the regional school as a juridic person or part of a juridic person is problematic. One can readily see that a school which is part of two or more parish juridic persons will face governance difficulties; conversely, if the school becomes a separate juridic person, its relationship to the supporting parishes is complicated.

A fourth type of school is one operated by a religious congregation or other independent body, such as a board of trustees. Religious congregations and trustees are not as directly related to the dioceses as are the members of governing structures of other schools. The independent school is a juridic person in its own right or is part of the juridic person represented by the religious congregation in that diocese.

The independent school owned by a Board of Trustees is becoming more common. Often a religious congregation owned the school and decided (usually in the face of limited finances and dwindling vocations) to withdraw congregational support from the school. If the congregation owned the property, the leadership often sold the school to a lay board of trustees with a provision that if the property and buildings were no longer used as a school, the property would revert to the congregation. Like the other types of schools mentioned, these are subject to the authority of the bishop in matters of faith and morals. Canon law requires that the bishop exercise supervision over the religious education programs of schools and those who teach in such programs. Independent Catholic schools and their board members must understand and accept the bishop's authority in these matters; to attempt to act in a manner contrary to the wishes of the bishop could place a school's continuation as a Catholic school at risk.

There is a small but growng number of independent Catholic schools that have dropped the word "Catholic" from their official titles. Literature may identify them as, for example, "St. Sebastian's School, an independent school in the Catholic tradition." It is important for boards of such schools to understand that one cannot be both truly Catholic and completely independent. To be a Catholic school requires that the authority of the bishop, as outlined in canon law, be recognized. Before a decision to drop "Catholic" frm a school's name is made, the ramifications of such a step should be seriously examined. There is no evidence to indicate that a civil court would allow a school to call itself "Catholic" against the directive of the bishop of the diocese in which it is located.

Many consultative boards function like boards with limited jurisdiction. The present movement towards government by collegiality and consensus sometimes results in little, if any, formal vote-taking; therefore, in practice, it is often difficult to distinguish between consultative boards and boards with limited jurisdiction.

Catholic School Boards and the Law

The Catholic school board has an important legal responsibility. It is crucial that board members understand that power is vested in the board as a body, not in individual members. Board members must understand what the role of the board is—the development of policy. Even if the policies have to be approved at a higher level, board members must understand their role in terms of policy.

Policy is usually defined as a guide for discretionary action. Thus, policy will dictate *what* the board wishes to be done. Policy is not concerned with administration or implementation; that is, the board should not become involved in *how* its directives will be implemented or *who are the* specific persons to implement them. For example, a board might adopt a policy requiring that all teachers employed be state-certified. The board should not be concerned with *which* teachers a principal decides to hire. Such questions are administrative ones; they are to be dealt with by the principal who is the chief executive officer of the school and also the chief executive officer of the board. Administrative decisions are the day-to-day management choices of the principal. It is crucial that everyone understand these distinctions from the outset.

Generally, boards will set policies in the major areas of

program, finance, and personnel. The board may also have responsibility in the area of plant maintenance. A board approves the budget, approves programs, sets tuition, sets hiring and dismissal procedures, and possibly oversees school facility planning. The board would also monitor the programs, the budget, and the implementation of policies. The principal would certainly suggest policies and would perhaps write the first draft of policies. The board approves the policies, the implementation of which is the principal's responsibility.

When tensions arise, board members must keep their responsibilities to the diocese and to the Church in view. If a board member cannot support a policy (and support does not necessarily mean agreement; it does mean a willingness to live with and not to criticize the decision), then change must be sought through the appropriate channels. A board is not free to adopt a policy at variance with that of the diocese. If change cannot be achieved and a board member still cannot support the policy in question, then the person's only real choice is to resign from the board. The board member has to remember that the board's responsibilities are really twofold: (1) to develop policies and (2) to support the persons and activities that implement those policies.

Disagreements should be left in the board room. Board members should remember that, as individuals, they have no real power. The power is vested in the board acting as a body. Becoming involved in internal school conflicts only weakens the authority of both the board and the administrator. The principal, however, should keep board members informed about problematic or potentially problematic situations so that board members will be able to respond in an intelligent manner if they are questioned.

Canon law governs all aspects of the Catholic school. Thus, Catholic schools and board members have no authority to act outside the provisions of canon law. But within those provisions, boards have great freedom so long as no civil laws are broken. Catholic school board members have much greater latitude in the governance of their institutions than do their public school counterparts.

The 1987 text, authored by the Chief Administrators of Catholic Education and the National Association of Boards of Education of the NCEA, *A Primer on Educational Governance in the Catholic Church*, adopts two main models for boards of Catholic schools that are owned by dioceses and/or parishes: consultative boards and boards with limited jurisdiction. In the past, terms such as advisory and policy-making have been used. Some independent schools and schools owned by religious congregations may still use the term "advisory board." An advisory board's function is to give advice; there is no obligation on the part of the one to whom it is given to take that advice.

A consultative board is one generally established by the pastor or by diocesan policy. This board has responsibilities for the development and/or approval of policies. The pastor has the final authority to accept the recommendations of the consultative board. This model is probably most effective when the pastor and principal are members of the board and are in regular attendance at meetings. If the pastor regularly decides not to follow the decisions of the board, members could view their role as useless. Thus, even though such a consultative board is, strictly speaking, advisory, the school's best interests would be served if the board is able to use a consensus model of decision-making whenever possible. Consensus does not mean that everyone agrees that a certain decision is the best possible one; rather, consensus means that all members have agreed to support the decision for the sake of the school.

A board with limited jurisdiction has been defined as one "constituted by the pastor to govern the parish education program, subject to certain decisions which are reserved to the pastor and the bishop" (CACE/NABE, p. 27) This type of board would have, in both theory and practice, more autonomy in decision-making than would the consultative board because the pastor has delegated decision-making power to the board with limited jurisdiction.

Schools owned by religious congregations or by boards of trustees may have either consultative boards or boards with limited jurisdiction. The board of a school owned by a religious congregation would relate to the administrator of the religious congregation in the same manner as a parish school board would relate to a pastor.

Persons serving on school boards often have questions concerning their personal civil liability if an individual should sue the school board. Historically, the doctrine of charitable immunity protected Catholic schools and those persons associated with them; as discussed in Chapter One, this protection is, for all intents and purposes, largely unavailable in modern courts.

Some states have passed laws which specifically protect members serving on boards of non-profit organizations, such as religiously affiliated schools, from civil liability. These laws presume *good faith* on the part of the board member; that is, a person is expected to act in the best interests of those served. Good faith is a traditional defense to most claims against board members in the public and private sectors. However, it must be frankly stated that plaintiffs will often allege bad faith in an attempt to defeat the defense. If bad faith is proven, the board member will probably not be immune from liability. Further, these laws granting immunity could be struck down by courts on a public policy theory: that is, public policy demands that individuals retain their rights to seek remedies for wrongs and that the state not pass laws that restrict those rights.

Board members must understand that they may be held personally liable if they knew or should have known that a certain policy violated a person's rights. In these days of increasing litigation, board members need liability insurance. As a matter of justice, dioceses and other school owners should obtain and fund such protection for persons serving on boards. If this protection is not available, board members should consider obtaining their own coverage.

Board members cannot presume that they have absolute immunity from liability. The best protection from a lawsuit is the effort to act always in accordance with justice. Board members should be offered some in-service education in the legal aspects of board membership. The diocesan attorney will be able to provide information concerning the laws of a given state and appropriate advice when questions concerning legal aspects arise. (The 1988 NCEA text, *A Primer on School Law: A Guide for Board Members in Catholic Schools*, by this author, may be helpful.)

The Principal's Rights and Responsibilities

As indicated above, the principal has the basic legal right to administer the school. No one should interfere with that prerogative lightly. The principal is entitled to the support of the bishop, the superintendent, the pastor, and the board. If, for serious reasons, any one or more of those parties cannot support the principal and an acceptable compromise cannot be reached, the principal or the differing party may have to leave the situation. In any event, all parties have the obligation to support one another publicly and to address differences in the appropriate forum.

Principals have numerous responsibilities, many of which are not found in any document. The safest course might be for a principal to assume responsibility for everything in the school. Like the bishop and the pastor, the principal may delegate decision-making powers to other persons, but the responsibility cannot be delegated. If a lawsuit is brought against a school and/or a teacher, it is extremely likely that the principal will be sued as well.

A principal has two main legal responsibilities: (1) policy formation and communication of rules and policies and (2) supervision of teachers and other personnel. Almost every activity a principal does can be placed under one of these two categories.

Even though school boards and pastors may have the final responsibility for ultimately approving policy, the principal plays an essential role in developing it. The best models for policy development are ones that either (1) have the principal write the first draft of the policy and bring it to the board or to a committee for discussion and revision or (2) have the principal serve as a member of a committee developing policy in a given area or areas. It is important that both pastor and board recognize the principal as the educational expert in the school and utilize that expertise to the fullest extent possible. Once a policy is adopted, principals communicate it and provide for its implementation.

One of the principal's most serious responsibilities is the supervision of teachers. It is crucial that everyone understand that supervision and evaluation of personnel are the principal's responsibilities. The principal is supposed to ensure that the best possible educational experience is given to students. In reality, supervision is quality control for the school.

Supervision of personnel is not simply a determination that persons are performing their jobs in an acceptable manner. It is also job protection for the teacher. If a principal does not supervise a teacher, and allegations are made against the teacher's competency, the principal will have no evidence to use in support of the teacher. If a teacher is faced with a malpractice suit, the principal is the person best-equipped to assist the teacher in refuting those charges. The principal's supervisory data will provide the necessary evidence.

The principal's legal responsibilities will be considered in greater depth in the remaining chapters.

CHAPTER THREE

RIGHTS AND DUTIES OF PARENTS AND STUDENTS

The most basic right of students in a Catholic school is the right to receive an education. The corresponding right of parents is to have their child receive an education. While the statement may appear obvious, it is important for everyone to remember that schools exist for students. Students do not attend school to provide employment for principals and teachers. This fundamental purpose of schools should be the principle by which all administrative and faculty actions are judged. Anything that interferes with the education of students should not be tolerated, whether that interference originates with parents, teachers, or students. The philosophy of the school should clearly state that education is the main purpose of the school.

Catholic school administrators, like all other school administrators, face the challenge of respecting student rights, while upholding discipline and order. Common law and common sense indicate that persons and institutions responsible for the education of youth are expected to hold students to appropriate standards of behavior. As the previous chapter indicated, the main source of the law governing Catholic school/student or parent conflicts is contract law. Nonetheless, the Catholic school administrator and teacher need to understand the Constitutional protections available in the public sector. Recent decisions have indicated that courts, utilizing contractual doctrines of fair play, can require Catholic schools to provide protections that are very similar to those required in the public school. Thus, despite the clear distinctions between public and private schools and the sound theory on which these differences are based, developing applications of the law in practice diminish these lines of demarcation considerably.

Student discipline is, of necessity, a major concern for Catholic schools. Without rules and a reasonable implementation of rules by administration and faculty, order would cease to exist, and schools would be unable to perform their function of education.

Several legal writers suggest that it is common law practice to notify someone of the charges against that individual and to give the person an opportunity to respond before imposing punishment. The English common law of private association, which protects members from expulsions contrary to natural justice, has also been held to apply to private institutions.

The concept of fundamental fairness is closely aligned to common law and is often invoked on behalf of students in Catholic schools. Sometimes used as a definition of due process, fundamental fairness is a broader concept than Constitutional due process. Fundamental fairness has its roots in the dictates of the Bible and other religious documents; it denotes a kind of "golden rule" approach—"do unto others as you would have them do unto you."

Almost all cases concerning student and parent rights in public schools involve the legal concept of Constitutional due process. Although Constitutional due process is required in the public schools and not in private schools, administrators may find knowledge of due process and its implications helpful in the development and implementation of rules, procedures and policies. Some historical background concerning due process is necessary if Catholic schools are to develop policies consistent with its demands.

The democratic principle of due process has its basis in the theory of social contract. Plato was among the first to articulate the theory which was substantially developed in more modern times by Locke and Rousseau: "The justification for the state's existence, according to Locke, was based on its ability to protect those rights better than individuals could on their own" (LaMorte, 1977, p. 32.) Locke's ideas are reflected in the Declaration of Independence which guarantees "certain inalienable rights, among these are life, liberty, and the pursuit of happiness." The Fifth Amendment to the Constitution guarantees that no person shall "be deprived of life, liberty or property, without due process of law." The Fourteenth Amendment extends that guarantee to the actions of individual states and protects people against arbitrary state action: "No state shall make or enforce any law which shall abridge the privileges or immunities of the citizens of the United States; nor shall any State deprive any person of life, liberty or property, without due process of law, nor deny to any person within its jurisdiction the equal protection of the law" (Amendment XIV, Section 1, The Constitution of the United States, adopted 1868.)

Title 42 of the United States Code, Section 1983 (the Civil Rights Act of 1871) protects persons whose individual constitutional rights are denied by state authorities. Section 1983 applies to persons acting upon the receiving end of actions "under color of state law." The actions of private individuals who are not in some way functioning as agents of the state are not governed by Section 1983 or by the provisions of the Fifth and Fourteenth Amendments. The decision handed down in the *Civil Rights Cases* (1883) states that the actions of private individuals do not fall under the domain of the Fourteenth Amendment unless substantial state involvement can be demonstrated.

Therefore, as indicated earlier, Catholic schools generally cannot be required legally to provide Constitutional due process protections unless state action can be found in the school or unless such protections are guaranteed by contract.

Due process demands fairness. Persons expect that parties to a lawsuit will be treated fairly by the judge and/or the jury: anyone accused of a crime will be told what it is that individual is alleged to have done (notice); one will be given a hearing or trial by an impartial party; the accused will be able to confront accusers (cross-examination) and call witnesses on one's own behalf. These expectations have been defined as "procedural due process."

Procedural due process has also been defined as a question: What process is due? What procedures are followed? Are they reasonable? Are all persons treated fairly and, insofar as possible, in the same way? Are there clear procedures that persons can expect will be followed?

Traditionally, courts have held that there are two types of due process: procedural and substantive. The concept of substantive due process is somewhat more difficult to understand than is the concept of procedural due process. Its root word, *substance*, might be helpful in understanding. You cannot violate someone's substantive due process rights unless the "substance" of which one is to be deprived is one to which the person had an existing right in the first place. The U.S. Supreme Court in the 1972 case *Board of Regents v. Roth*, involving the non-renewal of a one year teaching contract, declared:

> To have a property interest in a benefit, a person clearly
> must have more than an abstract need or desire for it. He
> must have more than a unilateral expectation of it. He
> must, instead, have a legitimate claim of entitlement to it.
> It is a purpose of the ancient institution of property to
> protect those claims upon which people rely in their daily
> lives... It is a purpose of the constitutional right to a hearing
> to provide an opportunity for a person to vindicate those
> claims. (p. 577)

This quote is extremely important to keep in mind when one begins to consider the rights of students and parents in Catholic schools and the responsibilities of Catholic schools in protecting those rights. The *Roth* case provides direction for the Catholic school administrator who might be tempted to think that, if a right cannot be found in the federal Constitution, one need not be too concerned about its protection. In *Roth*, the court clearly stated that the Constitution does not create property interests; that such interests are created and governed by the independent and separate entity which can be considered the source of the interests, such as state law or contract law.

Although Catholic school administrators are not required to follow Constitutional due process procedures, there is much to be learned from cases alleging deprivation of Constitutional rights in the public school. It would seem that the Judaeo/Christian ethic would require that at least the rudiments of due process be afforded parents and students in Catholic schools. Surely the scriptural mandates on which Catholic education rests would govern Catholic schools if the United States legal system had never evolved. Due process would seem to be a goal of any institution purporting to prepare students for life. Deprivation of rights without an opportunity to be heard is not fundamentally fair. The days of announcing, "All students whose names are on the board will stay after school, and there will be no discussion of the matter," are clearly over. Parents and students are right to demand Christian due process.

Student Discipline

Although contract law is generally held to apply in cases involving disputes between students and Catholic schools, traditionally courts have provided very little protection to students and parents on the basis of that law. Historically, courts have looked to catalogues, handbooks and other policy statements of schools as the basis for the contract. Such clearly seemingly ludicrous situations as the 1928 dismissal of Syracuse student for not being a typical Syracuse girl have been upheld in the light of catalogue or other written statements by the institution giving itself the right of dismissal without offering reasons *(Anthony v. Syracuse)*. It seemed as that contract law gave all the rights to the school and few, if any, to the student. Courts, as well as schools, have assumed students guilty until proven innocent. If contract theory is to assist the granting of due process in Catholic schools, it seems that schools must be compelled somehow to include some sort of due process procedures in their regulations. Such a task, historically, has been one courts have been loath to assume, as it might be construed as unlawful governmental interference in private affairs.

The doctrine of *in loco parentis*, while no longer successfully argued in the majority of public school cases, is still a powerful protection for the Catholic school, if appropriate limitations are understood:

> Because schools operate under the concept of *in loco parentis* (school authorities stand in the place of the parent while the child is in school), rules and regulations are permissible if their objective is consistent with the proper functioning of schools, they are reasonably related to educational goals, and they ensure a proper atmosphere conducive to learning. However, the *in loco parentis* concept has never meant that schools have the same disciplinary authority as parents. There have always been some limitations imposed in this regard (Chamelin and Trunzo, p. 75).

After the 1960s and the student rights cases litigated, many lawyers and educators declared *in loco parentis* to be dead, or at least, terminally ill. However, if parents can expect that teachers and school officials will stand in their place in providing for the safety of their children, it follows that school officials have the responsibility and the right to make reasonable rules, to provide for their implementation, and to impose appropriate sanctions when students do not follow the rules.

What is considered an acceptable procedure in a Catholic school may not be deemed Constitutional in a public school. The previously mentioned *Geraci* case hints that the lines between acceptable public school and acceptable private school procedures are not completely clear-cut; the *Geraci* court discussed "fundamental fairness" as analogous to Constitutional due process. In any consideration of discipline in the Catholic school, it is important to keep the *Geraci* findings in mind. It is much easier to make and implement fair rules from the outset than to try to undo damage resulting from poorly constructed and/or unfairly implemented rules.

Most school officials and lawyers would agree that the best school law, is, like medicine, preventive. The best defense to a lawsuit is having tried to follow the right course in the first place. Catholic school officials must realize that despite their best efforts in any and all areas of school life, they may well face lawsuits. All schools must look carefully at their rules and procedures to insure that they are reasonable, fair and consistent or else face the possibility of incurring the problems and expense of being sued.

E. Edmund Reutter, Jr. (1978), after an analysis of hundreds of cases, offers six minimum essentials for developing enforceable rules of conduct. These essentials, as relevant today as they were when written, are: (1) the rule must be published to students; (2) the rule must have a rational legitimate educational purpose; (3) the rule must have a rational relationship to the achievement of the stated educational purpose; (4) the meaning of the rule must be reasonably clear; (5) the rule must be sufficiently narrow in scope so as not to encompass Constitutionally protected activities along with those which may be proscribed in schools; and (6) if the rule infringes upon a Constitutional right, the compelling interest of the school in the enforcement of the rule must be shown.

While the fifth and sixth rules do not apply to Catholic schools, the other four are certainly valid and the last two may well be worth considering when developing a Catholic school handbook. Although a Catholic school is not bound to protect the Constitutional freedoms of parents and students, administrators would be well advised to know what those freedoms are in the public sector and to be prepared to offer some reasonable rationale for rules adopted that are not protective of those freedoms. For example, Catholic schools may require students to wear uniforms or to adhere to a strict dress code. The expression of viewpoints contrary to the teachings of the Catholic Church can be forbidden. Catholic schools may demand that students participate in religious exercises. These types of restrictions can easily be justified in the Catholic school.

Catholic school administrators should keep in mind Reutter's statement of essentials in developing rules. The previously mentioned dress code might serve as an example. If a uniform must be worn, the administrator must publish that fact to students and parents; it would be advisable for the school handbook or some official communication to give some reason for wearing a uniform (to promote discipline and to foster pride in being a student of the particular school, for example), and to mention the fact that wearing the uniform does, indeed, achieve that purpose. The meaning of "wearing the uniform" should be specific; for example, the official communication should make clear what the uniform is and when it is to be worn. If the above conditions are met, then the four essentials Reutter mentions would be satisfied.

It is the responsibility of the principal to develop the rules, to promulgate them, and to supervise their implementation. A principal must be sure that students and parents know the rule (uniforms must be worn) and that staff is enforcing the rule. If, through the negligence of staff or administration, students honestly don't know of the existence of a rule, they can hardly be held accountable for not following the rule. If teachers are responsible for implementation of rules, it is important that principals supervise that implementation. Principals should strive for the consistent enforcement of rules; although as the 1976 case *Flint v. St. Augustine High School* indicates, just because a rule has not been enforced consistently does not mean it can never be enforced.

Flint involved two young men expelled from a Catholic high school for a second violation of a no smoking rule. Although the handbook clearly provided for such disciplinary action, no one had actually been expelled for such an offense prior to this time, although other students had been guilty of the same offense. The justices stated that they regretted the school's decision but that, under the doctrine of judicial restraint, they had to respect the school's decision if it acted within the scope of its authority. The court stopped short of saying that the Catholic school could arbitrarily dismiss students at will when it stated: "That is not to say that due process safeguards can be cavalierly ignored or disregarded. But, if there is color of due process that is enough" (p. 234) Although the court found for the school in this case, one can easily see that consistency would have provided the school with an even stronger defense; certainly, fairness would seem to require that all schools attempt to be consistent in their enforcement of disciplinary policies.

The importance courts rightfully place on the development, promulgation, and implementation of rules is significant. Since handbooks and other written agreements can be construed as part of the contract existing between the school and its students and their parents, it is important that, as far as possible and practical, rules be in writing.

Courts look for evidence of good faith: did the institution have a rule? Was that rule promulgated? Did students and parents know of the rule? The court does not concern itself with the wisdom of the rule or even with the rightness or wrongness of the professional opinion of educators. The court is concerned only with the existence of a properly promulgated rule and with evidence that the institution acted in good faith according to the procedures it stated would be followed. As indicated earlier, courts will look for basic fairness in the execution of the contract existing between the student/parent and the school when the student is alleging that the school acted improperly in its imposition of disciplinary sanctions.

School officials, of course, should understand that they will never be able to write down everything a student could possibly do that might result in disciplinary action. Therefore, it is advisable to have some kind of "catch-all" clause such as "other inappropriate conduct." No court will expect a school to have listed all possible offenses, but courts will expect that *something* is written and that parents and students have a reasonable idea of the expectations of the school.

Corporal Punishment

A specific method of discipline, corporal punishment, is perhaps one of the most controversial topics in education today. Most states allow corporal punishment in public schools; only a very few prohibit corporal punishment in private and public schools. The 1977 Supreme Court decision *Ingraham v. Wright* is considered shocking by many persons. Two students in a

Florida public junior high school were paddled severely. Hospitalization and incapacitation resulted. The students brought suit, alleging a violation of the Eighth Amendment protection against cruel and unusual punishment. The court, however, ruled that school children were not protected as the Eighth Amendment protections applied only to prisoners. Therefore, reasoned the court, students in public schools were not entitled to procedural due process protections before the administration of corporal punishment.

In an interesting case after *Ingraham, Hall v. Tawney* (1980), the plaintiff pressed substantive due process claims. The *Hall* court decided that the *Ingraham* court did not address substantive due process, which it defined as ultimate bodily security. Although this case was not appealed to the Supreme Court, it raises some interesting questions. Future corporal punishment cases may very well use this same reasoning.

In a 1987 case, *People of Illinois v. Burdette Wehmeyer,* the court, using an accountability theory, found a principal guilty of battery of a student who had received a teacher-administered paddling witnessed by the principal. Interestingly, the teacher was acquitted. This case illustrates the doctrine of *respondeat superior,* let the superior answer. A superior can be held responsible for the acts of subordinates when performed within the line of duty. Corporal punishment is a broad term that encompasses more than "traditional" types of bodily punishment. Any punitive touching that results in harm to the student can be corporal punishment. Although there are no Eighth Amendment Constitutional protections for students in schools, educators can be found guilty of civil wrongs such as assault and battery if students are harmed as a result of punitive bodily contact. The *Ingraham* court, while declining to apply the Eighth Amendment to the case, stated that the students were free to pursue other legal remedies.

Two recent cases indicate that the controversy continues. In the 1990 Texas case, *Fee v. Herndon,* the court ruled that reasonable corporal punishment does not conflict with the due process clause. Echoing *Ingraham,* the court referred the student to other civil and criminal remedies and refused to support a Constitutional due process claim. The court did note, however, that excessive corporal punishment could be deemed child abuse.

In a 1990 Wisconsin case, *Thrasher v. General Casualty Co. of Wisconsin*, the court sought to determine whether throwing or pushing a student into a blackboard exceeds acceptable limits of corporal punishment. The court declined to find Eighth Amendment protections and rejected a claim that the teacher's action constituted an unreasonable seizure under the Fourth Amendment. The court refused to grant judgment for the teacher and remanded the case to the lower court for a determination of whether the student's substantive due process right to be free from unnecessary bodily harm had been violated.

Thrasher illustrates the notion that corporal punishment can be defined as any punitive touching. Thus, case law and developing case law raise the possibility that corporal punishment in all schools will become too risky as a means of discipline—in terms of legal ramifications for educators. The Catholic school is generally not governed by the same rules as the public school in regard to corporal punishment. However, the above-cited cases should provide any educator with food for thought. Catholic school personnel are not immune to civil tort cases or criminal charges of assault and battery if corporal punishment results in injury to the student.

Catholic school principals, like public school officials, might be well advised to propose other means of discipline than physical ones, both from the standpoint of avoiding lawsuits and from the standpoint of good psychology.

Suspension and Expulsion

Suspension and expulsion are usually last line strategies in student discipline. Both from the desire to act fairly and from the need to protect one's self and one's school legally, it is important to have sound policies and procedures in place when suspending and expelling students. The Catholic school is no exception.

Public school legal analysis can offer insights to Catholic school personnel. Drawing upon the principles articulated in public school cases, two writers, Chamelin and Trunzo, offer the following guidelines for disciplinary situations leading to suspension and/or expulsion:

1. A serious punishment like suspension or expulsion cannot be imposed for a minor infraction of rules or for the kind of conduct for which other students in the past have received only mild punishment.

2. The right to adequate notice of charges requires that a student be told in person the nature of the accusation, the school rule involved, and evidence against him or her where suspension or expulsion is a possible sanction.

3. As a general rule only a principal, superintendent, or school board can suspend. Teachers normally do not have this authority.

4. Where due process requires a suspension hearing, the hearing must be given before suspension unless the continued presence of the student in school poses a danger to persons or property or an ongoing threat of disrupting the school. In such cases, notice and hearing should follow as soon as practical.

5. As a general rule the length of the proposed suspension will govern the degree of formality under which the hearing is conducted.

6. The authority of schools to punish students for a rule violation which the student did not know existed will be determined by the courts on the basis of the severity of the violation, the reasonableness of the rule and whether the student should have known of the existence of the rule.

(Chamelin and Trunzo, p. 78)

The above stated principles should be helpful to any educator, public or private, in attempting to establish suspension and expulsion rules that are both fair to the student and protective of the institution's right to, and need for, order.

In the previously cited case, *Bright v. Isenbarger*, the court paid little attention to the procedures followed by the school in the expulsion of two young women because the students' case relied on a state action theory which was rejected by the court. The events and procedures which resulted in the expulsion are, however, worth noting. The expulsion occurred because the students violated a closed campus rule for the second time. There was no contention by the students that they were innocent of the violation of the rule. Further, they had been given notice at their first offense that a second offense would result in expulsion. When the second offense occurred, they did meet with both the principal and the dean of discipline. It is important to note that, in effect, the students were given notice, a hearing and an opportunity to refute the charges before two persons. Thus, although the court never addressed the procedural due process afforded the young women, the rudiments of due process were met. Further, the principal told the students and their parents that they would be eligible to re-enter the school in the fall.

Although this case predates the *Geraci* case, it seems that the actions of the school officials met the requirements of fundamental fairness.

The previously mentioned *Flint* case, involving two young men expelled for the second violation of a no-smoking rule, demonstrates that the burden of proof is upon students to establish that school officials acted arbitrarily, capriciously, or in bad faith. The court was careful to state that Catholic schools do not possess the power to do anything they wish, regardless of the fairness or appropriateness of the action:

> Sufficient for our purpose here is the observation that private institutions like St. Augustine High School have a near absolute right and power to control their own disciplinary procedure which, by its very nature, includes the power to dismiss students.
>
> That is not to say that due process safeguards can be cavalierly ignored or disregarded. But, if there is color of due process—that is enough... That such judicial restraint

may have an unhappy and seriously disconcerting effect on the academic lives of these two young men causes us grave concern in view of the disciplinary decision to dismiss rather than suspend them. But an even greater concern would be caused by our failure to impose the judicial self-restraint that is called for in this case. (pp. 234-235)

As was stated earlier, the expelled young men did know of the no-smoking rule and had been given warnings. The problem was that the expulsion penalty had not been imposed on earlier offenders. In fact, the trial court had found in favor of the young men because of the seeming injustice of the inconsistency: "A written rule which, to the knowledge of students and faculty, has never been enforced over a period of years is not a rule at all" (p. 234). Although there is obvious merit in the statement of the trial court, the appellate court chose to exercise judicial restraint because there was a written rule and, in the higher court's opinion, the administration had the right to impose the graver penalty, even if it had not chosen to do so on previous occasions.

The *Flint* case serves two purposes: it illustrates the basic provisions of fundamental fairness in *procedures* and it demonstrates the problems that may arise for administrators when those procedures are not uniformly followed.

The contract between the school and the student and parents places obligations on the school, as well as on the student, as the 1981 case of *Bloch v. Hillel Torah North Suburban Day School* illustrates. The Bloch case involved the expulsion of a first grade student in mid-year from a private Jewish school. The school alleged that the child was expelled for excessive tardiness and absence. The child's parents alleged that the expulsion was in retaliation for the parents' role in combating an epidemic of head lice in the school. The school maintained that the remainder of the school year during which the expulsion occurred was the only amount of time covered by the existing contract. The parents argued that, according to usage and custom, the first year's contract bound the school to providing eight years of education.

The trial court found that the school was not bound to continue educating the child, even if a contract existed, because of the highly personalized nature of the educational services. However, the trial court declared that the parents could seek financial damages for breach of contract. The appellate court agreed with the trial court and gave the following explanation for refusing to compel the school to meet its contractual obligations for the remainder of the year:

> The reasons for denying specific performance in such a case are as follows: the remedy at law is adequate; enforcement and supervision of the order of specific performance may be problematic and could result in protracted litigation; and the concept of compelling the continuance of a personal relationship to which one of the parties is resistant is repugnant as a form of involuntary servitude... Applying these principles to the present case, we believe that the trial court properly granted summary judgement... Although we are cognizant of the difficulties in duplicating the personal services offered by one school, particularly one like the defendant, we are even more aware of the difficulties pervasive in compelling the continuation of a relationship between a young child and a private school which openly resists that relationship. In such case, we believe that the trial court exercised sound judgment in ruling that plaintiffs are best left to their remedy for damages. (p. 977)

This interesting case raises several issues. One involves the nature of expulsion. From the facts presented in this case, it seems that the school had adequate reasons for dismissal (tardiness and excessive absence.) The parent argues convincingly that the school is punishing parental, not student, conduct. Although a determination of the "real" reasons was not considered necessary by the court, the case does illustrate the problems that can occur when a school wishes to rid itself of a parent and uses the conduct or misconduct of the child (however valid the disciplinary action may be) to achieve that end. It must be frankly admitted that there are occasions when the behavior of parents renders any meaningful school/home relationship impossible. An example might be a parent who consistently refuses to cooperate with the policies of the school. Schools wishing to ensure the ability to control such situations may insert a provision such as the following in their parent/student handbook: Parental cooperation is essential for the welfare of students. If, in the opinion of the administration, parent behavior seriously interferes with the teaching/learning process, the school may require parents to withdraw their children and sever the relationship with the school. Obviously, this type of action is very drastic and should be undertaken only after other attempts at conflict resolution have failed.

A second important issue raised by *Bloch* is that of damages for breach of contract. If a Catholic school is found to have wrongfully dismissed a student, the school will not be required to re-enroll the student. Rather, a court will assess financial damages, which may be considerable.

Breach of contract is an issue also raised in the private school expulsion case of *Wisch v. Sanford School, Inc.*(1976). This case contained facts similar to those in *Flint.* A seventeen-year-old student was dismissed for smoking marijuana in a dormitory bedroom. The plaintiff had no history of previous disciplinary violations. The record indicated that other students had been caught smoking marijuana but were not dismissed. The school handbook clearly stated that use of narcotics was grounds for suspension or expulsion from school. The plaintiff alleged that the school's action was a breach of contract because she was not afforded the same procedural safeguards and treated in the same manner as other students in previous similar disciplinary matters. The court declared that there was a contractual relationship between the plaintiff and the private school and further stated that terms may be implied from the contract in addition to express terms. One of those implied terms could govern disciplinary procedures. The court declined to find any irregularity in the treatment of the plaintiff; the school handbook allowed, but did not require, the expulsion of students involved in the use of illicit drugs.

Finally, the plaintiff sought to prove an interesting contention, that the school violated its *in loco parentis* responsibilities by expelling her. The court rejected the argument and stated that no school's responsibilities can be construed as being so like a parent's that expulsion can never be a remedy for student misconduct.

Thus, it can be seen that courts look for basic fairness in the execution of the contract existing between the parent/student and the school when the student alleges that the school is acting improperly in its imposition of disciplinary sanctions.

One of the most significant cases to date is the previously cited *Geraci* case. A review of the facts will aid in an understanding of the court's decision. Mark Geraci was a junior in good standing at a Catholic high school. His current tuition was paid and a deposit had been made on his senior year tuition. Mark was expelled for helping a friend, who was a student in another Catholic school, gain access to the school and throw a pie in the face of a teacher during a final exam. He admitted: (1) that he had been involved in the idea from the beginning; (2) that he was supposed to collect money to pay the student, although he did not actually collect any money; (3) that he gave the student directions as to how to gain access to the school building and to the teacher's room; and (4) that he, in fact, had arranged transportation for the young man.

After the incident, Mark met with both the assistant principal and the principal. The president of the school also met with Mark and his father before the decision to expel was reached. The record indicates that the school officials were concerned for the student and his family but that their decision to proceed with the expulsion was in accordance with their promulgated rules and procedures.

Both the Geracis and the school officials agreed that the school handbook was part of the contract between the student and the school. The court scrutinized the handbook which contained the following disciplinary norms:

> The St. Xavier norms of conduct are predicated on two premises: first, that every student has the right to certain protections (such as the protection of his personal property,

the physical integrity of the facilities, an atmosphere condu-
cive to personal growth and development) and, second,
that every student has the duty to preserve those rights for
others. The underlying concept is not one of legalisms,
punishments, or discipline for discipline's sake. Rather, it
is one of personal and corporate privileges bound of necessity to personal and corporate responsibilities. Since no list
of norms can cover every situation, the administration
presumes common sense, mature judgment, and Christian
charity are the guides by which every St. Xavier student
should measure his actions...

The following offenses are grounds for expulsion: 1.
conduct detrimental to the reputation of the school.. 2.
immorality in talk or action (p. 149).

The court decided that Geraci had actually breached his
part of the contract; in the court's opinion, encouraging and
aiding someone in throwing a pie in a teacher's face is, in fact,
"conduct detrimental to the reputation of the school" and
"immorality in talk or action." Such "catch-all" phrases are
appropriate ways for school officials to provide for dealing with
offenses that aren't found in the usual list of inappropriate
behaviors. As educators are all too well aware, students often
think of things to do that one would never imagine. "Catch-
all" phrases protect the school from an argument that a student
can't be disciplined for a certain behavior because "it isn't in the
handbook."

The above cases may appear dated; however, there continue to be very few cases involving student discipline in the
private sector. These cases provide strong guidance for administrators and indicate the probable direction courts will take. It
would seem that Catholic schools (while preserving their
identities as Catholic schools) would be willing to be fair and to
follow equitable procedures. Indeed, the *Geraci* court insists
that fairness is part of the responsibility incumbent upon
Catholic schools as part of the contract with parents.

Recommendations

All Catholic schools should develop clear rules governing student behavior and clear procedures for dealing with misbehavior. Catholic educators must be concerned with being models of moral behavior; disciplinary polices and procedures must be examined in the light of Gospel principles and of the fundamental dignity that is the right of all persons. While recognizing that a Catholic school does not have to grant Constitutional protections to students or follow legal guidelines given public schools by the courts, Catholic school officials would, nonetheless, do well to consider those guidelines when developing their own.

The beginning point for rules' development should be the school's philosophy. Principals must ensure that there is a clearly-written philosophy that informs on all the activities of the school. The philosophy must be viewed as a living document, not as something that was written once and has been put away somewhere to be brought out when the occasion requires it. No teacher should be employed unless the teacher has read the philosophy and has agreed to support it. At least once a year the faculty should consider and discuss the philosophy. If the philosophy no longer fits the lived reality of the school, the document should be changed. Parents and students should understand, and be able to articulate, the philosophy. Even very young children can be brought to some understanding of philosophy: "At our school we try to treat each other the way Jesus would treat us." The life of the school should be seen as flowing from the philosophy. Courts may analyze rules to see if they are consistent with the philosophy.

For example, if a school philosophy states, "We believe students are in a formative stage of life and, therefore, the purpose of discipline is growth, not punishment," but the school handbook lists some twenty or thirty reasons why a student can be expelled, it would seem that the documents are inconsistent.

If rules are clearly written, there is less likelihood that serious problems will arise when penalties are imposed. A rule stating, "Students are not to be late for class" could be considered vague; a rule stating, "Students arriving after the bell rings will be marked late," is much clearer and less open to debate.

Whenever possible, rules should be written, a requirement supported by common sense reasons. It is easier to display the written rule when emotions run high than to insist that "at the beginning of the school year, you were told thus and such." "Catch all" phrases, such as "other inappropriate conduct" should be added to a list of possible offenses, so that the school will be able to respond to inappropriate behavior that was not foreseen at the time the rules were written.

Every school should have some sort of written parent/student handbook. Schools should consider having parents and older students sign a form stating that they have read the rules and agree to be governed by them. A written handbook should encourage the school to strive for clarity in rule-making. Periodic evaluation should enable the school to make necessary changes in the rules. (Readers desiring more information concerning parent/student handbooks are directed to the NCEA publication, by this author, *School Handbooks* published in 1989.)

When considering the development of disciplinary guidelines and procedures, Catholic school officials must be aware that there is a time investment involved. If students are allowed to tell their side(s) of the story, the educator is committed to spending time with students. The benefit should be obvious: students perceive persons in authority as trying to be fair and will internalize the values that are modeled. If students see an educator behaving in a manner that is respectful of their dignity, they may be more likely to afford that same respect to others. This type of behavior will ensure that a school and its officials are acting according to "fundamental reasonableness" and, in the case of litigation, will offer a sound defense.

Catholic educators should commit themselves to notice and a hearing in any disciplinary situation; in this way, the school acts in a fair and moral manner. This commitment means that the students are told what they did that was wrong and are given an opportunity to present their side(s) of the story.

Somewhat more extensive procedures should be developed if the penalty is suspension. One-day suspensions should have the minimal requirement that the disciplinarian be involved and that the parents be notified. Longer suspensions should involve written notification specifying the charges and stating the time and place of the hearing. Cases in which the possibility of expulsion exists require written notification and a more formal hearing at which the student should be able to confront the accusers. Careful documentation should be made in all disciplinary proceedings.

The right of the student to legal counsel in suspension and expulsion hearings is a controversial topic. Catholic educators should understand that there is no legal requirement that a Catholic school permit legal counsel to be present at a disciplinary hearing; however, if the school grants that privilege to one student, a court could require that all other students in similar situations be given the same benefit.

The presence of attorneys creates an adversarial atmosphere, of necessity, and may well lessen the possibility of Christian reconciliation. This author believes that Catholic schools should not allow the presence of attorneys at school hearings. Obviously, the decision to allow legal counsel in disciplinary proceedings is not an easy one. An administrator should weigh carefully the advantages and disadvantages and should consult with legal counsel before developing policy.

Although Constitutional due process does not apply to students in Catholic schools, courts do look for fairness in the school's dealings with its students. Some experts believe that private schools should follow at least minimal due process procedures because of the demands of simple justice. Patrick Folan (1969) comments: "It seems only just that [private school] students be afforded due process in dismissal procedures." (p. 30) It seems better to practice preventive disciplinary measures in one's rules and procedures than to test their validity in a court room.

The above recommendations may be helpful to Catholic educators as they attempt to develop, modify, and implement rules and policies. Ultimately, the guiding principle should be the desire to act in a reasonable, moral way consistent with the Gospel, one's philosophy, and the principles of common law.

CHAPTER FOUR

RIGHTS AND DUTIES OF TEACHERS

Just as the rights of students in Catholic schools are somewhat limited, so are the rights of their teachers restricted. As discussed earlier in this work, the protections of the Constitution do not apply. Unless state action can be demonstrated, Catholic school personnel can claim no protected activities under the Constitution and no due process protections under the Fourteenth Amendment.

Catholic school teachers do have rights. These are generally conferred by the contract or agreement existing between the school and the teacher and so, the law of contracts governs the employment situation. State statutes may confer other rights. Additionally, teachers may be said to hold rights under the common law. Common law principles, referred to by Black as those principles "... which derive their authority solely from usages and customs of immemorial antiquity" (p. 250), are obvious in theory, but somewhat more difficult to delineate in legal practice. What may seem to be a principle of common law to one administrator may not seem the same to another. One administrator may consider it immoral to dismiss a teacher for freely speaking about administrative practices; another administrator may deem dismissing a teacher for such a reason as perfectly acceptable and, indeed, courts have upheld such dismissals. (See the previously cited case of *Rendell-Baker v. Kohn*, involving a private school teacher dismissed for her exercise of free speech.)

Francis W. O'Brien, writing in *The Journal of Law and Education* about due process and the fact that the private school administrators can absolve themselves from any responsibility for providing due process to their employees, offers these observations as timely today as when written in 1974:

> The correlative of natural law or higher law is natural rights... Suffice it to say that man [*sic*] by reason of his intrinsic dignity should have freedom to perform certain actions and should also have immunity from compulsion to posit certain other actions that derogate from his dignity. This implies that other persons have a reciprocal inhibition forbidding them from interference with this freedom and with this immunity that cloaks all human beings. This inhibition does not arise from any constitution or private action. It is higher than either and therefore has been called the higher law. It comes not from conventions but from the nature of things and thus may be called the natural law. For some people its source is God; for others it is simply man's innate rights which perceives the proper order in human relations. Whatever position one takes, there is fairly universal agreement that all men deeply feel certain "can't helps" compelling them to that they "should" do certain things and refrain from doing other things... [T]here is an objective norm of action that is most consonant with human nature (pp. 186-87).

The natural law that O'Brien discusses can be practically equated with the concept of common law. Common law and/or natural law demand that persons treat other persons according to certain accepted standards of behavior. If one were to try to compile a listing of teacher rights in Catholic schools, one could look to the common law.

Personnel Issues

The last few decades have been times of great change for Catholic education. In less than thirty years the majority of teachers in Catholic schools has shifted from members of religious congregations to lay persons. Catholic institutions have had to confront the issues of paying appropriate salaries to teachers, providing some sort of teacher benefits, and developing legally sound policies and procedures.

These issues have compelled school officials to examine the legal soundness of actions and documents. Administrators attempt to match word with deed. Constraints must be balanced against the requirements of justice. One of those constraints is civil law. The law is a parameter inside which we operate. If we move outside the parameter, we can lose everything inside the parameter. Disagreements between Catholic school personnel and school officials cannot always be solved in the pastor's parlor. Some disagreements propel the participants to court.

Civil courts have great respect for organized religion and its internal laws. Canon law governs the existence of Catholic schools and their relationships with various persons and institutions within the church. All Catholic schools, whether owned by the diocese or not, are subject to the bishop in matters of faith and morals.

The Revised Code of Canon Law calls for subsidiarity and collegiality in relationships and structures within the church. Subsidiarity requires that persons having disagreements or complaints should seek discussion and resolution of the problem at the level closest to the problem. If this procedure became standard practice in Catholic education, an untold number of problems could be solved before major crises develop and lawsuits are filed.

Bishops, pastors, superintendents and other administrators will usually be upheld if challenged in a court because of the First Amendment's protection of freedom of religion. This protection is not absolute, however. The 1982 case of *Reardon v. LeMoyne*, involving four women religious in conflict with the diocesan office, illustrates this point. This case represents the first time a group of Catholic religious women brought legal action against Church officials in a civil court.

The four sisters were notified in February that the superintendent did not intend to recommend that their contracts be renewed. The superintendent so notified the parish school board which notified the sisters that their contracts would not be renewed because of the superintendent's objections. The sisters then requested a public hearing before the board. This request was denied on the basis that their situation was one of non-renewal and not of termination.

The crux of the problem seemed to be the language of the contract and the fact that the sisters signed the same contract as did the lay teachers in the school. The language was, at best, ambiguous; at one point, the contract indicated that it would terminate upon the retirement of the employee which was to occur at the end of the school year during which the employee attained his or her seventieth birthday. The policies also stated that if a contract was not to be renewed, the party was to be notified in writing and given well-documented reasons for the non-renewal. The contract contained a further provision that an employee faced with dismissal had a right to a hearing before the members of the parish school board. There was a further right of appeal to the diocesan school board. The sisters asked the court to interpret their employment contracts.

The trial court found that the court could exercise jurisdiction over the lay members of the school board and not over the superintendent and the bishop because of the doctrine of separation of church and state. However, the trial court stated that the plaintiffs would not prevail against the school board.

On appeal, the state supreme court found that the doctrine of separation of church and state did not preclude jurisdiction in non-doctrinal contract matters:

Religious entities, however, are not totally immune from responsibility under civil law. In religious controversies involving property or contractual rights outside the doctrinal realm, a court may accept jurisdiction and render a decision without violating the first amendment... It is clear from the foregoing discussion that civil courts are permitted to consider the validity of non-doctrinal contractual claims which are raised by parties to contracts with religious entities. This requires the courts to evaluate the pertinent contractual provisions and intrinsic evidence to determine whether any violations of the contract have occurred, and to order appropriate remedies, if necessary (pp. 431-32).

In essence, the state supreme court found that the trial court should have accepted jurisdiction over the bishop and the superintendent as well as over the school board members. Further, the state supreme court held that the trial court should have ruled on the requests made by the sisters. The trial court should have acted on the sisters' requests so that their rights would have been protected and, perhaps, their employment contracts would have been renewed.

In the end, the case was reversed and remanded to the trial court to order a hearing for the sisters. Subsequently, the sisters and the other parties settled out of court; the sisters did not regain their jobs. The *Reardon* court found that civil courts, while not allowed to interfere in purely doctrinal matters, did have jurisdiction over the civil employment contracts of religious. The days of religious superiors' directing a religious to leave quietly and move on to a new assignment are largely over—as well they should be. Whatever rights are afforded lay personnel should be afforded religious, also. Conversely, whatever rules govern personnel should be applied equally to faculty members belonging to religious communities, the clergy, and the laity. There is no room for a privileged class or a double standard in Catholic schools.

Employment Policies

Dioceses, parishes, and schools are responsible for developing policies that protect the contractual rights of personnel. A parish has a contract with its teachers, and the faculty handbook can be considered part of the contract. Contracts place certain obligations upon teachers, but they also place obligations upon the employer. It is important that the school's policies be in line with those of the diocese, especially in view of the fact that most teacher contracts bind the teacher to observe the policies and regulations of the diocese. In the case of a religious congregation or independently owned school, the governing authority should be sure that it has significant reasons if it chooses to deviate from diocesan policy. In a strictly legal sense, a non-diocesan Catholic school is not bound by every mandate of the diocese to its schools. However, since a school can call itself Catholic only with the approval of the bishop, it makes sense that Catholic schools would strive for *voluntary* compliance with diocesan policies, wherever possible.

Dioceses are certainly free to develop guidelines in addition to, or in place of, policies. Generally, a guideline allows more latitude on the part of the parish or school than does a policy. However, the dioceses should insure that parishes, boards, pastors, and principals understand what is intended by the guideline: how binding is it? Are certain guidelines more binding than others? In some dioceses, there are no educational policies *per se*—there are only guidelines. Diocesan personnel should be in contact with the bishop who, in terms of canon law, is the only lawgiver, to be sure that diocesan handbooks reflect his wishes and that all relevant parties are made aware of the binding power of policies.

Policies become extremely important in the area of hiring procedures. These procedures must be in line with the requirements of civil law. Pre-employment inquiries carry the potential for violation of a person's rights. Administrators want to gather as much job-related information as possible, but at the same time invasion of privacy must be avoided. There are at least four areas of impermissible inquiries, first outlined by Horton and Corcoran: (1) questions concerning marital status and the family situation; (2) questions, which are not job-related, regarding personal history; (3) questions concerning associational activities; and (4) questions regarding irrelevant educational and work history, *etc.* It should be noted, however, that questions which are impermissible before employment may be asked after employment.

In Catholic schools there are legitimate concerns about providing for stability on faculties and about insuring that persons who are hired will have good attendance. Administrators may not, however, ask a woman if she intends to have children or whether baby-sitting will be a problem. Inquiries as to numbers of children and/or marital status are not permitted.

Job-related questions are allowed; some examples might be, "Is there any condition or situation that may cause you to have a problem with regular attendance?" or "Are you a Catholic in good standing with the Church?" Another approach would be to have an option section on the employment application; this section could ask marital status and numbers and ages of children, but the person could choose not to answer it. Questions regarding arrests and criminal records must be worded carefully. A person may have been arrested but never convicted. Many attorneys recommend a question such as, "Have you ever been convicted of a crime involving moral turpitude?" Some examples could be given, such as rape, murder, and felony convictions involving injuries of any kind to another person. If a person answers "yes" to such a question, that individual should be asked to provide the details. It is advisable to state that conviction of such a crime is not an automatic bar to employment and that the hiring officials will consider the nature of the offense and the connection between that offense and the position sought.

Applicants should be asked to sign a statement giving permission for background checks. Many states now have laws requiring all persons who work in schools to be fingerprinted and the fingerprints checked against records of criminals convicted of felonies and/or misdemeanors. In the absence of such state law, a diocese may wish to set its own policy regarding fingerprinting. In addition, if a physical examination is required, a person's medical records should be kept separate from all other records.

Dioceses should consider having one employment application for all schools. General questions could be followed by specific sections for prospective teachers, secretaries, cafeteria or custodial workers. Such a common form would ensure that all applicants for all positions are evaluated on a fair and equal basis.

Teachers and other professional staff members should be offered contracts. The contract should incorporate the faculty handbook and the diocesan handbook. For example, a clause might state, "The teacher agrees to uphold the policies and procedures of the school and of the diocese. The teacher agrees to uphold the teachings and laws of the Catholic Church, the final arbiter of which is the bishop."

Catholic Schools and Discrimination

Federal anti-discrimination laws are binding on Catholic schools. Most schools now file statements of compliance with federal anti-discrimination laws with appropriate local, state, and national authorities. It is almost unheard of for a Catholic school to be accused of discriminating in regard to students. Unfortunately, it is not as uncommon to hear of alleged discrimination concerning personnel.

Catholic schools cannot discriminate on the basis of race, color, national origin, age and disability (if, with reasonable accommodation, the needs of the disabled person could be met.) Sex can be used as a condition of employment only if the school has a tradition of being single sex and only teachers of that sex have been hired. Catholic schools can discriminate on the basis of religion, and Catholic teachers can be given preference in hiring. Catholic schools and those responsible for the administration of Catholic schools must exercise caution and avoid even the slightest suggestion of inappropriate discrimination.

The 1980 case, *Dolter v. Wahlert*, illustrates. Ms. Dolter, an unmarried teacher in a Catholic school, became pregnant. The principal later rescinded her contract, although evidence indicated that he had known that male faculty members had engaged in pre-marital sex but had not disciplined them. The court rejected a "separation of church and state" defense and ruled that the issue in this case was not premarital sex but sexual discrimination. In a somewhat humorous footnote to the case, the court states, "The court certainly can take judicial notice of the fact that under the present physiological laws of nature women are the only members of the human population who can become pregnant" (p. 270). Anti-discrimination legislation can impact Catholic schools because the government has a

54

compelling interest in the equal treatment of all citizens. Compliance with statutory law will be required if there is no less burdensome way to meet the requirements of the law. In *Dolter* the court was careful to state that the non-renewal of the teacher's contract would have been upheld if men known to have engaged in premarital sex had been treated in the same manner. The problem was not the school's position on premarital sex, but the fact that rules had been unfairly applied on the basis of sex.

Age discrimination laws prohibit discrimination against persons in the 40-70 age bracket. It is not permissible to ask potential employees their age prior to employment. The only permissible question is, "Are you between the ages of 18 (the age at which one becomes an adult in the eyes of the law) and 70 (the age at which the law permits mandatory retirement)"?

It is not uncommon to find Catholic school administrators who say, "I prefer to hire a person right out of college or with little teaching experience. That way we don't have to pay as great a salary." True financial exigency can be a reason for choosing a less experienced applicant. If the applicant were to challenge the school in court, the school would not be in a very strong position to assert financial exigency if arguably non-essential expenses were paid. For example, a principal who declined to hire a teacher based on "no money to pay" and who subsequently bought a new $15,000 copier would probably be found guilty of age discrimination.

The existence of a disability in an applicant can be problematic for Catholic schools. Section 504 of the Rehabilitation Act of 1973 applies to schools receiving any sort of federal financial assistance. Most Catholic schools receive lunch subsidies, block grant monies, or some sort of indirect assistance. It has been argued that these types of assistance are not significant; however, few Catholic schools would want to be part of a test case. It should be noted that the Americans with Disabilities Act, which will take effect shortly, further defines acceptable employment conduct. The Disabilities Act states that a person cannot be denied employment simply because of a disability. A disabled individual (or a person with a handicap) is generally defined as one who has a physical or mental condition that significantly affects one or more life functions, such as movement, speech, sight, etc. Disabled people must be given fair employment consideration if, with reasonable accommodation on the part of the employer, they can perform the duties of the position. A job application or an interviewer should not ask, "Do you have a handicap?" but rather, "Is there any reason why you would not be able to perform the responsibilities of this position?"

Some Problematic Areas

One especially problematic area regarding discrimination is AIDS. While there are guidelines concerning the acceptance and continuance of students with AIDS in both the public and private sectors, it is hard to find guidance for employment issues in the public sector.

Lower courts have supported the right of individuals with AIDS to employment as long as the disease does not interfere with their work, and no one is placed in danger. The difficulty often comes, not with meeting those requirements, but with dealing with persons who discover that an applicant or employee has the disease. There are no easy answers. A Catholic school, acting in accordance with the Gospel, cannot turn away individuals with this twentieth-century disease. Legally, a Catholic school that would attempt to deny admission or employment to a person with AIDS, may find itself defending a lawsuit charging the school with discrimination. One could anticipate a result such as the one in the previously cited case, *Bob Jones v the United States.* The government, having a compelling interest in the equal treatment of all persons, could deny the Catholic school tax-exempt status, the situation which occurred at Bob Jones University; a natural consequence could be the endangerment of the tax-exempt status of all Catholic institutions.

This discussion of AIDS should indicate to school officials the importance of sound education on the topic, adequate legal consultation, and clear policies and procedures written *before* a situation has to be addressed.

The issue of homosexuality is not so difficult from a legal standpoint. While homosexuals have been afforded discrimination protections in employment, courts have not ruled in favor of active homosexuals who have sought to begin, or continue, employment in an institution owned and/or operated by a religious group that opposes homosexuality on religious grounds. Obviously, the Catholic Church is one such institution officially condemning active homosexuality. The Catholic school administrator must understand that it is the active nature of the homosexuality, not the homosexual orientation, that is the problem. Persons who realize they are homosexual but decide to live a chaste lifestyle should not be at any legal risk. A person who is involved in a homosexual relationship is in a different category. That individual is acting in a manner opposed to the teachings of the Catholic Church and so has violated the employment contract. School officials cannot and should not monitor the private lives of employees *unless* the private life becomes a source of, or possibility for, scandal. The situation involves a very fine line, obviously. Homosexuality is another area in which policies and procedures should be developed before the situation presents itself.

The issue of upholding the teachings of the Church, of being a practicing Catholic or a member in good standing of another religion, and of upholding the policies of the school and/or diocese can be problematic. Who defines what is a practicing Catholic? The situation of the divorced Catholic contracting a second marriage without an annulment of the first marriage is perhaps the one most often faced by Catholic school administrators. Even if the person in question is convinced that he or she is acting in good conscience in contracting a second marriage outside the church, there is little doubt that the person is, objectively speaking, in violation of church law and hence, a possible source of scandal. This situation is not a problem from the standpoint of terminating the employment of a person who violates church law. The religious organization clearly can terminate the employment of one who violates religious norms. The problem is the lack of consistency from diocese to diocese, from school to school, and even within schools. It is simply not just, and it may not be legal to treat such persons on an individual basis. All persons and institutions, whether private or public, are expected to be fair. How can an employer claim to be fair in dealings with employees if it treats the same infraction differently, depending on who is involved? It is difficult to defend dismissal decisions on religious grounds if one person is dismissed for an action and another, having acted in the same manner, is retained. These principles hold in any case in which religious principles are involved and concerns about discrimination exist.

In the case of *Holy Name v. Retlick*, a Catholic school principal sought to deny unemployment benefits to a teacher whose contract was not renewed because she married a divorced man before he was granted an annulment of his first marriage. This case was complicated by the fact that the evidence indicated that the principal had suggested to the teacher that she live with the man so as to avoid the public scandal that a marriage could cause. The court found it difficult to accept an argument that the teacher's marriage was grounds to deny unemployment benefits when the principal was willing to accept the teacher's living with a man to whom she was not married. The court found that marriage is not misconduct and that the teacher was entitled to unemployment benefits. If there had been a clear policy in place and the principal had adhered to it, this case would probably have never been in court. The case also illustrates the fact that principals should never assume that they can speak as private persons in such situations; any words will very likely be used as evidence against them and can incriminate their institutions as well.

A second case, *Bischoff v. Brothers of the Sacred Heart* 416 So.2d 348 (La. Ct.App. 1982) was brought by a new teacher whose contract was canceled prior to the opening of the school year when the principal discovered that the plaintiff had been divorced and remarried and, hence, was not considered a Catholic in good standing. The school had three faculty members in similar situations, but it argued that those people did not teach religion, and the plaintiff was being hired to reach religion. The plaintiff stated during the trial that "he didn't divulge his marital history because he knew [the principal] would not have hired him under those circumstances" (p. 351). The court found for the school; part of its reasoning was the fact that the plaintiff had been a Catholic seminarian for six years and he knew that he would not be a suitable candidate for a religion teacher in a Catholic school. Although the school prevailed, its position would have been strengthened if it had a written policy on the subject of divorced teachers who remarry without Church approval.

Bischoff also raises questions of fairness that are not easily answered. Is it just to hold religion teachers to a different standard than that for all other teachers? Is a religion teacher really different from other teachers, or are all teachers role models and, hence, teachers of religion?

Courts may be moving to a more conservative position as the 1990 Pennsylvania case, *Little v. St. Mary Magdalene Parish*, indicates. Ms. Little, a divorced, non-Catholic, tenured teacher brought a civil rights action against the school when it did not renew her contract after she, without obtaining an annulment of her first marriage, entered into a second marriage with a Catholic man. Ms. Little alleged that the parish's action was a violation of her rights under both Title VII of the Civil Rights Act of 1964 and state law, as well as a breach of contract. Catholic schools, like other religious organizations, are exempt from claims of religious discrimination under Title VII. Ms. Little argued that, by employing a non-Catholic, the school was waiving its right to the exemption. The court declined to find such a waiver.

Ms. Little had signed contracts containing a "Cardinal's Clause" which allowed the parish to terminate a teacher's employment for "public rejection of the official teachings, doctrines or laws of the Roman Catholic Church." The parish maintained that her conduct, though permissible in her religion, violated the Cardinal's Clause. In granting summary judgment for the parish, the court ruled that "[a] religious organization's right to make employment decisions based on religion exists throughout the employment relationship, not just during the hiring process" (p. 601). This case suggests that the right of Catholic schools to hold teachers, regardless of religion, to strict standards of conduct compatible with the teachings of the Catholic Church can be upheld.

It seems that the safest legal course for schools and dioceses to follow is to develop policy and to enforce it. As difficult as it may be to dismiss employees, it is unfair to pick and choose who will be held to a policy. Justice demands that officials construct policy that is applied equally to all.

Breach of Contract

As indicated throughout this work, the prevailing law in Catholic schools is contract law. A contract is an agreement between two parties each of whom incurs a detriment and derives a benefit from the contract. A teacher agrees to teach (a detriment in that one is unable to perform other employment during that time, and the teacher receives a benefit (salary, *etc*). The school incurs a detriment (payment of salary) and receives a benefit (the students are being taught).

Breach of contract occurs when one party fails to perform. When a Catholic school is involved in litigation with teachers, the court will examine the provisions of the contract. *Weithoff v. St. Veronica School,* an early (1973) but significant case, illustrates. The school terminated Weithoff's contract after her marriage to a priest who had not been laicized. She had signed a contract of employment which bound her to observe the "promulgated" policies of the sponsoring school. A policy requiring teachers to be practicing Catholics had been adopted by the governing body, but the policy was filed and never published to teachers. Therefore, Ms. Weithoff alleged that the school's dismissal of her was a breach of contract. The court agreed and ordered the school to pay damages, the remedy for breach of contract in the private sector.

Weithoff illustrates the importance of contract language. Had there been no clause requiring "promulgation," there is a very strong possibility that the school would have won this case; the court might well have ruled that a person who teaches in a Catholic school should expect to be held to the requirements of church law.

In a case similar to *Weithoff, Steeber v. Benilde-St. Margaret's High School* (No. D.C. 739 378, Hennepin County, Minn. 1978), the court upheld the non-renewal of the teaching contract of a teacher who remarried after a civil divorce without obtaining a Church annulment. The difference in this case was that the court upheld the right of the school to have a policy requiring staff members to be practicing Catholics. In *Weithoff* the school failed to prevail in court because of the contractual terms it had imposed on itself and its own failure to adhere to them. Breach of contract can be committed by either party to the contract—the school or the teacher. It is generally conceded, however, that it is futile for a Catholic school to bring breach of contract charges against a teacher who wants to terminate a contract; to compel a person to teach would be tantamount to involuntary servitude or slavery. Courts have stated that since replacements are readily available, a school sustains no injury; without an injury, there can be no lawsuit. As frustrating as this reality can be for principals, it is simply a fact of life in the Catholic school.

Some persons suggest including liquidated damages clauses in contracts; a teacher who breaches a contract must pay a fee toward the cost of finding a replacement. The labor laws of most states do not permit withholding monies from salaries, so a school could be forced to pursue a small claims action which might result in a teacher's paying an amount as low as one dollar a week. Thus, a school might be well advised to forego the liquidated damages scenario.

Schools are responsible for developing policies that protect the contractual rights of personnel. A court can consider the faculty handbook to be part of the contract. Contracts place certain obligations upon the teachers, but they also place obligations upon the employer. It is important that the school's policies be in line with those of the diocese, especially in view of the fact that most teacher contracts bind the teacher to observe the policies and regulations of the diocese and/or other sponsoring organization.

Discipline and Dismissal

Most cases involving teachers in both the public and the private sectors are concerned with teacher dismissals and/or the non-renewal of contracts. Obviously, a decision to dismiss or not to renew the contract of a teacher is one that an administrator should not make lightly, and it is one that should be made only after other attempts at discipline of the faculty member have been made.

Although the Constitutional protections afforded public school teachers are not granted Catholic school teachers, both sets of teachers are protected by contract law. Administrators must honor the provisions of the contract or be able to give a legitimate reason for breaking the contract. Courts will scrutinize contracts to ensure that the provisions of the contract have been followed. While a Catholic school contract may be far less involved than a public school contract, it is nonetheless a contract.

Catholic school administrators should be familiar with the laws governing the dismissal of public school teachers in their states. The laws can serve as guidelines in developing policies and procedures for Catholic schools.

A quick survey of the laws of any state will reveal the problems involved in defining the causes for dismissal. For example, most states allow dismissal for incompetency. But what is incompetency? Who decides what it is? When is it serious enough to warrant dismissal?

Generally, states consider the following as grounds for dismissal. *Incompetency* is a term that can encompass any of several conditions: physical or mental incapacity which is permanent and incurable (although federal law prohibiting discrimination must be observed); lack of knowledge about the subject matter one is contracted to teach or lack of ability to impart that knowledge; failure to adapt to new teaching methods; physical mistreatment of students; violation of school rules; lack of cooperation; negligent conduct; failure to maintain discipline; and personal misconduct in or out of school that affects teaching performance. It is readily apparent that incompetency encompasses a wide range of behaviors.

Insubordination is generally the willful refusal to abide by the rules or the directives of superiors. It can be distinguished from incompetency in that an incompetent person may be involved in the same behavior as an insubordinate employee, but the incompetent person is not assumed to be willfully violating duties and rules.

Unprofessional conduct is also a broad concept. It may be the same behavior as personal misconduct. However, while all personal misconduct can probably be construed as unprofessional conduct, not all unprofessional conduct is personal misconduct. For example, it might be considered unprofessional conduct to discuss school matters at the dinner table if one's school age children are present, even if the children are forbidden to repeat the conversation outside the home; it would be difficult to put that behavior in the same category as personal misconduct, such as sexual offenses or arrest for driving while intoxicated.

Immorality is listed in the statutes of many states as grounds for dismissal. Different communities, however, have different standards of morality and those standards change with time. Delon and Bartman (1979, p. 65) observe, "It is not surprising that persons who lose their positions or certification on this ground [immorality] often urge the courts to declare it unconstitutionally vague." Case law indicates that courts differ in their interpretation of what constitutes immorality and what constitutes unfitness to teach. In the public sector, at least, some courts have held that performing an immoral act may not be justification for terminating employment unless it can be demonstrated that the immoral act or public knowledge of the immoral act impairs one's ability to be an effective teacher. (See

Board of Education of Long Beach Unified School District of Los Angeles County v. Jack M. 566 P. 2d 602, Cal. 1977 which involved a public school teacher who was arrested and subsequently dismissed for an isolated incident of sexual misconduct. The court ruled that the one incident did not constitute proof of unfitness to teach.) Standards of "fitness" and "unfitness" are changing. Possession of marijuana in one's home might not be a cause to dismiss a teacher unless it can be shown that the behavior affects teaching performance. Today it may be fairly easy to show that a teacher convicted of driving under the influence has had teaching effectiveness impaired.

The Catholic school and its officials have a well-defined body of Church law to guide them in determining what is moral and what is not. Nonetheless, interpretations among reasonable people can differ considerably. Thus, it is extremely important the appropriate officials anticipate problem areas and plan policy accordingly. Just as a principal cannot foresee everything a student might do that could warrant expulsion, officials will not be able to compile a list of immoral actions applicable to every situation that may present itself. Discussion and planning before a problem appears can help to ease the difficulties that are always inherent in cases in which teachers are alleged to have acted in an immoral manner.

"Catch all" clauses such as "any other just reason" can be found in many state statutes. These clauses allow for action in situations that may not seem to be covered under any rule. For example, if a public or private school teacher were found innocent by reason of insanity of a serious crime, such as murder or rape, a school could possibly impose dismissal even in the absence of a pertinent statute or policy. The fact that the teacher had indeed killed or raped someone could render school officials within their rights to dismiss.

Courts will generally apply the "whole record test" in teacher dismissal cases except in situations such as criminal conviction or other gross misconduct. If an administrator is seeking to dismiss a teacher for incompetence, the dismissal will probably not be upheld if it is based on a single incident. The court will consider the whole record of the teacher in determining whether the dismissal was proper.

Policies governing non-renewal of contract and dismissal from employment should be in place in all Catholic schools. Non-renewal of contract and dismissal from employment are not synonymous terms. Non-renewal of contract does not carry the same connotation and stigma that dismissal from employment or "being fired" does. Sometimes, the terms are used synonymously. Indeed, the way many contracts are written throughout the United States, teachers in Catholic schools may face non-renewal of contract every year because the contract contains a clause such as, "This contract expires June 30 unless renewed." In many of these situations, there is little real difference between non-renewal of contract and dismissal; if a principal wants to dismiss a teacher, the teacher is not offered a contract for the coming year. In *Reardon* the superintendent attempted to characterize the sisters' termination of employment as a "non-renewal" rather than a "dismissal." It is not wise to try to evade termination issues, especially in a case like *Reardon*, in which the plaintiffs had each spent between five and twelve years in the school, by attempting to call termination of contract a non-renewal and, therefore, not subject to whatever protections may apply to dismissed employees. A contract can identify the difference between non-renewal at the end of a school year and termination during a school year or at the end of a school year, but it would be advisable to seek legal counsel in constructing such a document. Administrators might also want to consider if that kind of verbal "hairsplitting" is really the fair thing to do. *Reardon* is a case in which the plaintiffs might have been found to possess *de facto* tenure, a concept discussed below.

Tenure considerations, while very different in the public and private sectors, are important in teacher dismissal. Almost every public institution has some provision for granting teacher tenure. While tenure is commonly considered to mean that a teacher has an expectancy of continued employment, it is important to remember that an expectancy is not an absolute guarantee. Gatti and Gatti define tenure: "Tenure is a job security device. Tenure does not guarantee continued employment, but it does provide that a tenured teacher or administrator may not be removed from his or her position without specific or good cause" (pp. 378-379). Tenure then is job protection. It is the assurance that if a teacher performs duties in a reasonable manner, then that teacher can expect to be re-employed. Tenure is granted in the public school usually only after a probationary period during which the teacher is periodically evaluated. State statutes specify a given period of probation.

It would seem that in most dioceses tenure would not exist. One exception would be those dioceses that have unions. A 1979 Supreme Court decision, *NLRB v. the Catholic Bishop of Chicago*, held that Catholic schools did not have to allow union representation. Unions that were in place in Catholic schools prior to this ruling were not affected by it. However, the tenure issue is not a totally moot point in Catholic schools. Private sector employment is said to be "at will." Employers generally may hire and fire whom they please. Discrimination is one area in which employers may not fire with impunity. Recent case law in private industry indicates that courts may be moving away from absolute at will employment. One can usually dismiss employees for no reason or for a good reason but not for a bad reason. Discrimination would be a bad reason.

Dismissal at will may not be an option if a school has a policy whereby a teacher can expect continuing employment after a given number of years. Even if no policy exists, *de facto* tenure (tenure in fact) could be held to exist if an expectation of continuing employment is documented. If teachers in a Catholic school are routinely offered contracts after a given number of years of employment, *de facto* tenure could be found to exist. Although no court has yet held that Catholic schools can be compelled to reinstate wrongfully terminated teachers, courts have ordered Catholic schools to pay damages to teachers who have successfully argued that their contracts had been breached. Such was the appropriate remedy in the previously mentioned *Dolter* case involving the pregnant unmarried Catholic high school teacher.

Public School Cases

Public school cases provide points of comparison for Catholic school situations. Public school teachers who are dismissed and bring suit generally do so on the grounds that their Constitutional freedoms have been violated. Whatever other issues (such as statutory regulations or contract considerations) may also be pressed, Constitutional freedoms are generally an issue. Previous chapters have dealt with the concepts of substantive and procedural due process as protected under the Fifth and Fourteenth Amendments.

The other Constitutional freedoms besides due process that are generally at issue are those guaranteed by the First Amendment. Public school teachers cannot be dismissed because of their exercise of free speech. Unless the exercise of free speech somehow substantially interferes with the running of a school, free speech must be protected. If a teacher who has engaged in controversial speech is to be dismissed, it must be demonstrated that the dismissal would have occurred even if the protected speech had not been uttered. Five major United States Supreme Court cases alleging First Amendment violations in the public schools are: *Perry v. Sindermann* 408 U.S. 593 (1972); *Board of Regents v. Roth* 408 U.S. 564 (1972); *Pickering v. Board of Education* 391 U.S. 563 (1968); *Mt. Healthy v. Doyle* 429 U.S. 274 (1977); and *Givhan v. Western Line Consolidated School District* 439 U.S 410 (1979).

The United States Supreme Court has ruled that teachers have a Constitutional right to speak freely on matters of public concern. Teachers may not be Constitutionally compelled to relinquish First Amendment rights to comment on matters of public interest in connection with the operation of the public schools in which they work; they enjoy these rights as citizens. (cf. *Keyishian* 385 U.S. 589, 1967). Although the state does have an interest in regulating employee speech, this interest differs from the right the state possesses in regard to the speech of the general citizenry; a balance must be achieved between the interests of the teachers and the interests of the state.

The details of these public school cases are omitted in the interest of space, but the basic principles provide worthwhile considerations for the Catholic school administrator as well. If Catholic school administrators wish to limit the free speech of teachers within their employ, they would do well to develop a policy statement showing some rational basis for the policy. For example, it would be reasonable for a Catholic school to have a policy requiring teachers to uphold the doctrines of the Church. If a biology teacher were to make pro-abortion statements to students, a Catholic school would be justified in dismissal since abortion is contrary to Church teaching. What a court will construe as behavior which violates the teachings of a religion may depend on unforeseen variables, and an institution's position is greatly strengthened by a written rule.

Like student discipline cases, there are few private school teacher discipline cases as compared with those in the public school. If a teacher is going to sue a private school, it will probably be due to dismissal.

As the first chapter indicated, state action arguments will probably fail in the light of the U.S. Supreme Court case of *Rendell-Baker v. Kohn.* This case dismissed the argument of Ms. Kohn, the teacher, that the state's provision of up to 99% of this private school's budget constituted state action was rejected by the court, particularly in view of the fact that the dismissal action was not in any way related to funding issues. Thus, a Catholic school teacher who brings a cause of action for wrongful dismissal cannot expect to be helped by a state action argument. Generally, contract law is the basis for determining the outcome of Catholic school/teacher disputes.

The cases involving Catholic schools discussed above illustrate that administrators cannot hide behind First Amendment separation of church and state doctrine as a "cover" for any actions they wish to take. The courts have made it clear that they do have jurisdiction over the elements of a contract made with a religious entity, particularly over non-doctrinal issues. *Reardon* indicates that even members of religious congregations have civil contractual rights when employed by religious organizations.

The *Holy Names* case illustrates, that while courts will not rule on the rightness or wrongness of a given religious doctrine, they will look to see whether the *action* based on the doctrine is reasonable and consistent. The principal's suggestion that the teacher live with the man she intended to marry instead of contracting a civil marriage was imprudent at best and certainly did nothing to increase the school's ability to provide a reasonable defense.

The *Weithoff* case illustrates the need for clear policies that are disseminated to all. Weithoff prevailed solely because the school failed to promulgate the policy which would have prohibited her from marrying a priest and remaining a teacher in good standing at the school. *Steeber* and *Bischoff* indicate that the courts will hold the teacher accountable for knowing what is or is not acceptable behavior and will uphold the right of the Catholic school to dismiss those whose behavior is not acceptable.

The *Dolter* case establishes the right of the courts to intervene in sex discrimination cases. The *Bob Jones* case demonstrates that, since Congress has made racial discrimination a matter forbidden by public policy, courts will intervene in racial discrimination suits. These cases strongly suggest that all discrimination against candidates who, with reasonable accommodation can perform the duties of employment, will be struck down by the courts. The sole exception in Catholic schools is religion; Catholic schools may give preference in hiring to Catholics and may require support of the teachings of the Church as a condition of employment.

Documentation: Creating a "Paper Trail"

The faculty handbook and/or the employment contract should state, at least in general terms, the reasons for which a teacher may be terminated. The most important factor to keep in mind in any termination or non-renewal situation is documentation. The best protection against a lawsuit is a written record of the reasons and events leading to termination.

The principal should document all events that illustrate what it is that makes an employee ineffective or undesirable. Administrators should keep in mind that teachers and other professional employees may be doing an adequate job in the classroom but may still be behaving outside the classroom in ways that are unacceptable. Some examples might be excessive absenteeism, tardiness, lack of cooperation, etc. Documentation should describe behaviors and avoid judgments. It would be better to record, "Ms. Smith sent twenty students to the office for misconduct in a three-day period," than to state "Ms. Jones is having difficulty keeping order."

It is crucial that a principal have a "paper trail" indicating that the teacher was told of problems and given an opportunity to improve. One way to ensure appropriate communication and documentation is to follow a seven-point checklist when conferencing with teachers who present problems.

CHECKLIST FOR CONFERENCING WITH TEACHERS

(1) Enumerate precisely what is wrong and needs improvement.

(2) State that the school wants the teacher to improve.

(3) State what the school is going to do to help the teacher.

(4) Give a deadline at which time all parties will review improvement or lack thereof.

(5) Tell the employee that, if there is no improvement within the time frame stated, disciplinary action will result.

(6) Give the teacher a copy of the conference document stating the first five points and ask the teacher to comment on the document to ensure understanding.

(7) Have the teacher sign the document and add any comments he or she wishes to include; if the teacher refuses to sign, have another person witness that fact. (This other person should be another administrator or the pastor; if neither is available, a secretary could serve as a witness. Asking another teacher to serve as a witness should be avoided.)

Problems can arise when procedures aren't followed or when conflicting policies exist. In the *Reardon* case, part of the problem was the conflicting policy statements regarding the continuation of employment. The difficulties of inconsistency are obvious; administrators need to ensure that documents are consistent.

In keeping with fairness and due process considerations, dioceses and schools should develop policies requiring that a teacher facing suspension or dismissal be told of the charges and be given an opportunity to refute them. Some process for appeal should be in place. In many dioceses, the bishop is the last "court of appeal." In schools owned by religious congregations, the congregational governing board may serve in that capacity. The important point is that there be some avenue of appeal for a teacher who has taught in a Catholic school a length of time for which tenure would have been awarded in the public schools.

Although legal experts differ on the applicability of the doctrine of *de facto* tenure, there seem to be, to this author at least, biblical considerations. The Gospel demands that dioceses and schools provide some minimal job protection for teachers and ensure that just termination procedures are in place in every school. If a Catholic school dismissed a teacher who has been working in that school for ten years, a court would look at the policies, procedures, and past practices of the school or school system. If teachers are routinely retained in the system after a certain number of years, there is the possibility that *de facto* tenure could be found to exist.

Some might argue that a teacher facing disciplinary measures up to and including termination should be allowed to have an attorney present at every stage of the process. There is no civil law requirement that this be done and, indeed, the presence of attorneys can often create an adversarial atmosphere and lessen the possibility of attaining some sort of Christian reconciliation. Policy-makers may wish to allow a person facing dismissal or non-renewal of contract the opportunity to bring a witness who is not allowed to speak.

Although Catholic schools are not bound by all the employment constraints that oblige public schools, knowledge of those constraints should aid Catholic school officials in developing policies that are fair and just. Simply because administrators are not legally bound to do something doesn't mean that they shouldn't do it if it seems the morally right thing to do. One should always ask: Is it the fair thing to do? Is it moral? Is that what I would want or expect someone to do to me if I were in the teacher's position? Is it the position Jesus would take? Sometimes it is difficult to balance legal and Gospel considerations, but such is the challenge facing Catholic schools and their leaders.

CHAPTER FIVE

SOME SPECIAL TOPICS

Torts

Tort cases are the most common form of legal action brought against educators. A tort is defined as a civil or a private wrong other than breach of contract. The four main types of educational tort cases are: corporal punishment; search and seizure; defamation of character; and negligence. Negligence suits outnumber the other three put together. Constitutional issues related to corporal punishment and search and seizure do not apply in the Catholic school. However, the legal consequences of defamation and negligence are the same in the public and private sectors.

Corporal Punishment

Chapter three offered a discussion of corporal punishment. Although some states permit corporal punishment, Catholic schools would be well advised to avoid it. While the administration of the punishment might not be illegal, injuring the child physically, mentally, or psychologically is. The risks of student harm and educator liability make corporal punishment a poor disciplinary choice in any school, but particularly in the Catholic school.

Search and Seizure

The 1985 Supreme Court decision, *New Jersey v. T.L.O.*, involved the search of a student purse in a public school. The search yielded marijuana; the police were notified and charges were filed against the student who was later found guilty of possession of a controlled substance. The student alleged that her Fourth Amendment rights protecting her against unreasonable searches had been violated. The Supreme Court declined to find such a violation in this case. The court stopped short of declaring that students had no Fourth Amendment rights in the public sector; rather, the court adopted a reasonable, rather than a probable, cause standard in public school searches. A public school official must have at least some reasonable rationale for conducting a search; "fishing expeditions" to discover what contraband might be present, without more reason, is not allowed.

New Jersey v. T.L.O. does not apply to Catholic and other private schools. Nonetheless, Catholic schools should have some kind of policy for searching students and/or seizing their possessions. Searching a student should require "more" cause than searching a locker.

Lockers and desks are school property and the school has every right to examine them and their contents. A school strengthens its position with students and parents by including a phrase such as the following in handbooks, "The school is co-tenant of lockers and desks and reserves the right to search them at any time without notice."

If a principal believes that a student is carrying a dangerous item on his or her person, the principal should ask the student for it. If the student refuses, the student can be asked to empty pockets, book bags, purses, etc. If the student still refuses, the principal must make a choice. Obviously if the principal believes that persons are in danger, the principal will have to take whatever action appears necessary to gain possession of the item. If the situation permits, the best course of action would appear to be to contact the parent and have the parent come to school and conduct a search of the child. Obviously, such a procedure is a serious one and should be undertaken only in appropriately serious circumstances. Where possible, principals should contact the appropriate diocesan personnel or attorney for advice.

Catholic schools and their personnel can be subject to tort suits of assault and battery and/or invasion of privacy if a student is harmed because of an unreasonable search. Carefully developed policies and procedures should guide any search and seizure; a common sense "balancing test" should be applied in each case: is this search and its possible effects worth finding whatever it is that school officials are seeking? For example, an exhaustive search for a student's lost dollar does not seem worth the effort. After asking if anyone has seen the dollar, the teacher would be well advised to lend the student a dollar, if necessary, than to disrupt the educational process by a search. If the student has lost an expensive piece of jewelry, the teacher might conduct a more extensive search. Approach is most important. Saying to students, "Let's all help Johnny look for his watch. Let's all look in our book bags to see if it could have fallen into one by mistake," while the teacher examines his or her own bag, avoids the trauma of students being singled out for accusation. The dignity of each student and a commitment to treat everyone the way the educator would wish to be treated should be guiding principles in any search and seizure situation.

Defamation of Character

Defamation of character is another type of tort that can face Catholic school personnel. Defamation is an unprivileged communication that harms the reputation of another. Defamation is a twin tort; it can take the form of slander, which is oral defamation, or libel, which is written. Some persons mistakenly believe that the truth is an absolute defense in defamation cases. While truth is an absolute defense in most such cases, it may not be in the case of an educator and a student or a principal and a teacher. Because of the serious responsibility educators have, they are generally held to a higher standard than are non-educators.

School officials should be concerned with protecting the good name of all in their schools. Administrators should exercise great care in keeping student and teacher records, as well as in more overt actions. It seems only just that an administrator would refrain from gossip or unnecessary derogatory remarks about teachers or students. The best advice for both teachers and principals is to be as factual as possible in official documents and to refrain from "editorial" comments. Whatever is written should meet the following three criteria: (1) it should be specific; (2) it should be behaviorally oriented; and (3) it should be verifiable.

It is better to say that a student has twenty absences, ten tardies and five disciplinary referrals to the principal's office than it is to write, "This student is a real problem, absent all the time and always in trouble."

Similarly, comments in teacher records should be strictly factual. Anything which is to become part of a teacher's file should be made known to that individual; in the case of any disciplinary action, the document should be signed by the teacher.

If there is no reason to have an item in an individual's file, it should be stored elsewhere. Official student files should contain only the following: the academic transcript; records of educational or related testing; an emergency sheet; and a health form. Everything else can and should be placed in another non-official file. Teacher files should contain: (1) transcripts; (2) employment application; (3) letters of recommendation for employment; (4) records of administrative observations and follow-up conferences; (5) evaluation forms, including self-evaluation forms; and (6) any disciplinary records, including written reprimands. It should be noted that disciplinary records are part of the teacher's file, but not of the student's file. Student disciplinary records should be kept separately; students are still in a formative stage and school officials should be extremely careful in storing information in an official file that could be harmful to the student. Should a serious situation exist that needs to be shared with another educational institution, parents can be asked to sign a form authorizing release of disciplinary records.

In these days of increasing litigation, most administrators are familiar with the problems of writing legally non-controversial recommendations for employees and students without sacrificing the truth. Further, most administrators have read recommendations that seem to be saying very little. Administrators must understand that no one has an absolute right to a recommendation. Teachers and students can be given letters verifying employment or enrollment and factual statements about employment duties or educational credits earned can be made. The guideline is to be as fair as possible. School officials should strive to be fair and respectful of the dignity of others in all communications, whether official or not, and to say only what can be shown to have some valid relationship to the professional situation. In so doing, school administrators and teachers protect themselves against possible lawsuits alleging defamation and/or invasion of privacy.

Confidentiality of Records

An issue related to invasion of privacy is confidentiality of records. If an educator follows the procedures outlined above, the risk of having problematic materials in student and/or teacher files is minimized. Permitting teachers and other employees access to their personnel files ensures the individual's knowledge of the contents of those files; hence, an individual would find it difficult to maintain either defamation or invasion of privacy actions if that individual authorized the access of another to the files, such as in a release of file contents to a prospective employer.

The content of student files should be released only to authorized persons. Even school personnel should be given access to student files only for appropriate school-related reasons. Parental signatures should be required before records are sent to anyone.

The issue of the non-custodial parent is a significant one today when so many students are not in the custody of both parents. Principals may often find themselves facing a non-custodial parent who wants a copy of the student's records or other information. The Buckley Amendment grants non-custodial parents the right of access to student records; this

Amendment binds public schools. There is a difference of opinion among legal experts concerning the applicability of this Amendment to the private school. Some scholars interpret the law as not affecting the Catholic school. Others believe that Catholic schools can be held to its requirements. There has been no case concerning the Buckley Amendment and Catholic schools decided in any court of record. It is this writer's opinion that Catholic schools should voluntarily comply with the law. If one chooses not to comply, one runs the risk of becoming a test case in the courts. There are common sense reasons for allowing non-custodial parents involvement in the lives of their children. Unless there is a court order to the contrary, a non-custodial parent should be allowed to discuss a child's progress and should be given unofficial copies of the report card, if requested. Of course, a non-custodial parent has no right of physical access to the child unless granted by court order.

Catholic schools would be well advised to include a provision such as the following in parent/student handbooks: "The school voluntarily complies with the provisions of the Buckley Amendment. Non-custodial parents will be given access to unofficial copies of student records and staff will be available to discuss the student's records, unless a court order providing otherwise is filed with the school." Another appropriate inclusion would be the requirement that divorced parents file a notarized copy of the custody section of the divorce decree with the school; such a procedure would help to protect the rights of everyone in the family.

Negligence

Negligence is the most common of all lawsuits filed against teachers and administrators. Even though negligence is the "fault" against which administrators must constantly guard, it is also the most difficult type of case about which to predict an accurate judicial outcome. What may be considered negligence in one court may not be considered negligence in another. It is much better, obviously, to avoid being accused of negligence in the first place than to take one's chances on the outcome of a lawsuit.

Since negligence is an unintentional act or omission which results in injury, a person charged with negligence is generally not going to face criminal charges. Persons who bring successful negligence suits are usually awarded money damages in an amount calculated to compensate for the actual injury suffered. It is possible, though rare, for a court to award punitive or exemplary damages if the court is shocked by the negligent behavior. In assessing whether a person's behavior is negligent, a court will use the "reasonable person" test: would a reasonable person in the defendant's situation have acted in this manner? "Reasonable" is whatever the jury or other fact-finder decides it is.

There are four elements which must be present before legal negligence can be found: *duty, violation of duty, proximate cause, and injury.* An examination of each of the four elements should prove helpful. First, the person charged with negligence must have had a duty in the situation. Students have a right to safety and teachers and administrators have a responsibility to protect the safety of all those entrusted to their care. Teachers are assumed to have a duty to provide reasonable supervision of their students. It is expected that administrators have developed rules and regulations which guide teachers in providing for student safety. Teachers will generally not be held responsible for injuries occurring at a place where or at a time when they had no responsibility. A student injured on the way to school normally will not be able to demonstrate that a teacher or administrator had a duty to protect students.

Administrators should, however, be aware of the fact that courts may hold them responsible for student behavior and its consequences occurring on school property before or after school. In one such case, *Titus v. Lindberg* (1967), a principal was found to be liable for student injury occurring on school grounds before school because: he knew that students arrived on the grounds before the doors were opened; he was present on campus when they were; he had established no rules for student conduct outside the building nor had he provided for the supervision of the students. The court found that he had a reasonable duty to provide such supervision when he knew students were on the property as a regular practice.

The *Titus* case illustrates the dilemma in which school administrators may find themselves. If a parent delivers a student to school at 6:30 A.M. and the school doors open at 7:00 A.M., is the administrator responsible for the student? How does the administrator provide for supervision? Should supervision be provided? If the rules state that no one is allowed on the grounds before 7:00 A.M., is the school simply encouraging students to congregate on public or private property other than the school's and what will be the school's responsibility for student behavior occurring off school property? It is important to keep in mind that the court will look at the reasonable nature of the administrator's behavior. Is it reasonable to expect that an administrator will provide for the supervision of students on school grounds no matter how early they arrive and how late they stay? Probably no court would expect an administrator to be present at 6:00 A.M.; however, the court will expect some policy or statement as to when students may arrive on campus, what rules they are to follow, and what kind of supervision will be provided.

Such problems are not confined to the early morning. Students who remain long after school is dismissed or who arrive early on non-school days for athletic or other practices also pose problems.

There are several possible approaches to this supervision problem. One is to post "no trespassing" signs and enforce a policy of no presence on school grounds outside specified times. If a student is on the grounds at a time when no supervision is provided, the parents should be notified. Appropriate warnings and penalties should be given. Parents could be required to withdraw a child from school after repeated offenses. Another approach would be to pay someone to provide supervision before and after school. Probably the best solution for elementary schools is to provide an extended care program. A policy could be implemented requiring that any child who is present in the school building or on the grounds at unlawful times will be placed in day care and the parents will be billed for the service. (The 1991 NCEA text, *Extended Care Programs in Catholic Schools: Some Legal Concerns*, by this author, may be helpful in developing and maintaining extended care services.)

Negligence cannot exist if the second element, *violation of duty*, is not present. Courts understand that accidents and spontaneous actions can occur. If a teacher is properly supervising a playground and one child picks up a rock, throws it, and so injures another child, the teacher cannot be held liable. However, if a teacher who is responsible for the supervision of the playground were to allow rock-throwing to continue without attempting to stop it and a student were injured, the teacher would probably be found to have violated a duty. Similarly, a teacher who leaves a classroom unattended in order to take a coffee break will generally be found to have violated a duty if a student is injured and it can be shown that the teacher's presence could have prevented the injury. If it can be shown that teachers often left students unattended while the principal, through inaction or inattention, did nothing about the situation, the principal has violated a duty as well under the previously mentioned doctrine of *respondeat superior*.

The violation of duty must be the *proximate cause* of the injury. The court or jury has to decide whether proper supervision could have prevented the injury and, in so deciding, the court has to look at the facts of each individual case. William Valente, in his text *Law and the Schools* (1980), has observed, "To be proximate, a cause need not be the immediate, or even the primary cause of injury, but it must be a *material and substantial* factor in producing the harm, 'but for' which the harm would not have occurred" (p. 351).

The tragic 1976 case of *Levandoski v. Jackson City School District* illustrates. A teacher failed to report that a thirteen-year-old girl was missing from class. The child was later found some distance from the school; she had been attacked and subsequently died. The child's mother filed suit against the school district and alleged that, if the child's absence had been reported, the murder would not have happened. The court found that no evidence existed proving a causal link between the violation of duty and the injury. Thus, the case failed in proximate cause. One can easily see how a slight change in the facts could produce a different ruling. Had the child been found dead on or near school property, a court might well have found that proximate cause exited. It is not the act itself which results in legal negligence; it is the causal relationship between the act and the injury. If the relationship is too remote, legal negligence will not be found. Any reasonable educator will try to be as careful as possible, of course, and not gamble on the "causal connection."

A well-known case which illustrates the concept of proximate cause is the 1982 case, *Smith v. Archbishop of St. Louis*. A second grade teacher kept a lighted candle on her desk every morning during the month of May. She gave no special instructions to the students regarding the dangers of lighted candles. One day a child, wearing a crepe paper costume for a school play, moved too close to the candle and the costume caught fire. The teacher had difficulty putting out the flames and the child sustained serious physical and resultant psychological injuries.

A second case concerning proximate cause is the 1971 Minnesota case, *Sheehan v. St. Peter's*, in which an eighth grade student lost an eye as a result of being struck by a rock thrown by another student. Evidence indicated that the teacher had brought the students to the playground and then returned to the school building; she did not reappear until after the injury. Evidence further established that students had been throwing rocks for some time before the student was struck. The trial court found the teacher negligent; her behavior, absenting herself from the playground, was the proximate cause of the injury. The teacher could not defend herself on a spontaneous injury argument (her presence would not have been able to prevent the injury), since the student was injured only after many rocks had been thrown. The court reasoned that, had the teacher been present, she would have stopped the activity before the student was injured.

The *Sheehan* case should not be interpreted as meaning that teachers can never leave students unsupervised. There are occasions when teachers can reasonably leave students alone. One such instance would be an emergency requiring the teacher to leave; courts have declined to offer a definition for "emergency." If an accident occurs during a teacher's absence, the court will decide whether the teacher's action was reasonable. In the 1969 case, *Segerman v. Jones,* a physical education teacher left her class unattended while students were doing push-ups. One of the student's feet hit another student's head and damaged her teeth. The appellate court found the teacher to be innocent of negligence as it ruled, under the spontaneity theory, that the teacher's presence might not have prevented the injury.

In determining whether a teacher's behavior is reasonable, a court might ask the following questions. Has the teacher given the students clear instructions as to how to behave when no adult is present? Is the teacher absent a reasonable length of time? (Five minutes seem reasonable; a thirty minute absence during which a teacher had a cup of coffee, made a phone call, and/or made copies would probably not be considered reasonable.)

In determining whether the principal would be liable for accidents occurring during a teacher's absence, a court might pose these questions. Has the principal developed a clear policy for teachers needing to leave classrooms? Has the policy been implemented? Has the principal supervised teachers to make sure that they are following policy?

In both *Smith* and *Sheehan,* the trial court discussed the concept of *foreseeability;* it was not necessary that the defendant have foreseen the particular injury but only that a reasonable person should have foreseen that some injury was likely.

Proximate cause can be tempered by the legal theories of contributory negligence and comparative negligence. Schools may use the defense that the injured student contributed to the harm. Gatti and Gatti have observed: "Contributory negligence is the oldest and most commonly used defense against negligence. Under this rule, even if a teacher or an administrator was negligent, he or she will not have to pay if the injured party was also negligent" (p. 127.) This concept has been replaced in the majority of states by that of comparative negligence. Courts, operating under a comparative negligence doctrine, attempt to determine each person's part in the action or inaction and, hence, each person's percentage of responsibility for the injury. Comparative negligence can result in a lower award of damages than would normally be given, if it can be shown that the student was responsible for a "percentage" of the injury. It is possible for an injured party to be considered responsible to such an extent that the school is exonerated from blame. Such a result was reached in the 1989 case, *Brown v. Tesack*. Two students removed partially used cans of duplicating fluid from a dumpster, carried them to the apartment complex in which they lived, played with them, and ultimately set them afire. A third child was severely injured when the fluid cans exploded. The injured child's mother alleged that the school's disposal of the fluid containers was negligent and thus, the school district should be liable for the injuries sustained by her son. The court discussed causation: "[N]egligent conduct is a cause-in-fact of harm to another if it is a substantial factor in bringing about the harm." The court found that the school had not breached its duty of care in disposing of the fluid; the actual cause-in-fact was the students' negligent misuse of the duplicating fluid. The school's action was not considered the proximate cause of injury. Thus, proximate cause is a complex concept. It is difficult to predict what a court will determine to be the proximate cause in any particular allegation of negligence.

The fourth element necessary for a finding of negligence is *injury*. No matter how irresponsible the behavior of a teacher or administrator, there is no legal negligence if there is no injury. If a teacher leaves twenty first-graders unattended and no one is injured, there is no negligence in the legal sense. Any reasonable person can see, however, that no one in authority should take risks that may result in injury.

In order to bring suit in a court of law, an individual has to have sustained an injury for which the court can award a remedy.

Courts follow the principle, "the younger the child, chronologically or mentally, the greater is the standard of care required." It might be acceptable to leave a group of high school seniors alone for ten minutes when it would not be acceptable to leave a group of first graders alone.

Most negligence cases occur in the classroom because that is where students spend most of their time. However, there are other areas that are potentially more dangerous than the classroom and, hence, a greater standard of care will be expected from teachers and administrators.

Shop and lab classes contain greater potential for injury and cases indicate that courts expect teachers to exercise greater caution than they would in ordinary classrooms. Teachers and administrators are further expected to keep equipment in working order and to keep the area free of unnecessary hazards. It is also expected that students will be given safety instructions regarding the use of potentially dangerous equipment. In the 1974 case, *Station v. Travelers Insurance Co*, school officials were found to be negligent when injury resulted from the use of a science lab burner that was known to be defective.

Athletics present another hazard, probably one of the most serious. Writers Clear and Bagley (1982) state the nature of the problem:

First, it must be assumed that litigation can and will arise from each and every [athletic] injury that occurs. This creates an awareness that much is at stake. Second, it must be believed that the only way to avoid liability for injury is to be completely free from cause relating to it. Third, no action can ever be taken or not taken which results in injury to a student. The first two stages are easy to reach; they are merely matters of belief. But the third is not so simple to attain, for it requires specific knowledge regarding both tort law and the sophisticated technical aspects of sports and sports injuries... It is sufficient to state that coaches owe athletes a standard of care that includes the following: (1) proper precautions to prevent injuries from occurring in the first place and (2) treatment of injuries that normally occur in a manner that does not exacerbate the damage that has already been done. This standard, additionally, is based on what the coach *should have known* regarding the sport and/or injury, as well as what was actually known (p. 185).

Even if every possible precaution were taken, the possibility for student injury during athletics is very high. Administrators have very real duties to ensure that: competent, properly trained personnel serve as coaches for teams; clear procedures are followed when accidents occur; there is no delay in seeking medical attention when needed; equipment and playing areas are as hazard-free as possible.

In developing and implementing policies for supervision of students, the principal must keep in mind the reasonableness standard and ask, "Is this what one would expect a reasonable person in a similar situation to do?" No one expects a principal or teacher to think of every possible situation that might occur. No one can foresee everything that might happen; but reasonable persons can assume that certain situations might be potentially dangerous. The teacher in the *Smith* case should have foreseen that second graders might be injured by an open flame; the teacher in the *Sheehan* case should have foreseen that leaving eighth grade students unsupervised on a playground might result in harm.

The best defense for an administrator in a negligence suit is a reasonable attempt to provide for the safety of all through appropriate rules and regulations. The best defense for a teacher is a reasonable effort to implement rules and regulations.

Field trips pose special problems with respect to negligence. Principals and teachers must exercise great care in providing for field trips in Catholic schools. Most legal experts would agree that field trips should have an educational purpose. If an accident were to occur, a school could much more easily justify an educational trip that one that is purely recreational in nature.

Parents should be required to sign a permission form that requests the school to allow the child to participate in the activity as well as gives permission for the participation. The form should also include a statement that the parent releases the school and its personnel from liability in the event of accident and/or injury. (A more complete discussion of field trip policies and procedures can be found in the publication, *School Handbooks.*)

Principals and teachers must understand that parents cannot sign away their children's right to safety. Those who supervise students are expected to act in a responsible, appropriate manner. Some people question the need for a permission slip, since liability can occur anyway. A properly constructed and signed form is the best protection a school can have should an accident happen. Permission slips are not absolute protection, but it ensures that parents understand that their children are participating in a field trip and that there are risks involved in any such experience.

Child Abuse Reporting

The failure to report suspected child abuse and/or neglect is a special kind of negligence. Educators who fail to report can incur both civil and criminal penalties. Every state has a law mandating that educators report suspected abuse and neglect.

Many law enforcement officials advise educators to report everything that a child tells them that could constitute neglect or abuse. These officials caution educators not to make decisions about what is and what is not abuse; police departments and social agencies are charged with that task.

Deciding to report is never easy. Teachers who have suspicions should discuss these immediately with their principals. Many schools follow a policy which involves the principal making the report. This is acceptable procedure and allows the teacher to achieve some emotional distance from the situation. Teachers must understand that, if for some reason, a principal refuses to make a report and the teacher sincerely suspects abuse, the teacher is legally obligated to report. The laws of most states protect teachers who make "good faith" reports, even if these reports later prove to be unfounded.

Educational Malpractice

Another special form of negligence is malpractice, a relative newcomer to the field of educational law. Black's *Law Dictionary* defines malpractice:

Professional misconduct or unreasonable lack of skill.... Failure of one rendering professional services to exercise that degree of skill and learning commonly applied under all the circumstances in the community by the average prudent reputable member of the profession with the result of injury, loss or damage to the recipient of those services to those entitled to rely upon them (p. 864).

Currently, malpractice suits are found in the public sector; this author knows of no cases brought against Catholic schools in any court of record. But the possibility of such a lawsuit certainly exists. The most often litigated type of educational malpractice involves an allegation that the student never learned to read due to the school's or the teacher's breach of duty. It is possible, however, for a student to bring such a lawsuit for failure to master any subject.

Students do not easily win these cases; nonetheless, teachers and principals should take all reasonable measures to protect themselves against allegations of malpractice. The first and best defense is, of course, performing one's duties to the best of one's abilities.

Records of supervisory visits to classrooms provide powerful support for a teacher who is forced to defend a malpractice suit. These records should provide evidence of the teacher's competence and instructional performance. Teachers should keep copies of all such records.

Finally, teachers can protect themselves by keeping careful lesson plans. If the school does not store lesson plans from year to year, the teacher should keep the plans in his or her own files.

Copyright Law

A final area of tort consideration is copyright law. The technological explosion of the past few decades has given educators much greater copying capabilities. With those capabilities comes a greater risk of violation of the copyright law.

Most educators realize that copyright law exists. If asked, many would reply that they know there are rules governing the copying of articles, books, computer programs, cassette tapes, and videotapes. For some individuals, the fact that apprehension and prosecution for breaking the copyright law are rare becomes a license to break the law. For others, their motive of helping students to learn is an excuse for failing to comply with the law.

Upon reflection, most educators would agree that copyright protection is a just law. Persons who create materials are entitled to the fruits of their labor; those who use author's creations without paying royalties, buying copies, or seeking permission to copy, are guilty of stealing. Educators may be tempted to think that copyright infringements and lawsuits are the exclusive domain of large institutions. Obviously, if a company is going to sue someone, it will seek a person or institution that has been guilty of multiple infringements so that larger damages can be won; it simply doesn't make good economic sense to sue someone who will be ordered to pay only a small amount of damages.

Sometimes, though, lawsuits are brought solely to prove a point. In the 1983 case, *Marcus v. Rowley*, two teachers were the litigants. One teacher had prepared a booklet for class use; the second teacher copied approximately half the pages and included them in her teaching materials. The amount of money involved was very small. Nonetheless, the court found the second teacher guilty of copyright violation; her use of the other's materials was not fair.

Section 107 of the 1976 Copyright Act deals with "fair use" and specifically states that the fair use of copies in teaching "is not an infringement of copyright." The "sticking point" is what the term "fair use" means. The section lists four factors to be included in any determination of "fair use":

(1) the purpose and character of the use, including whether such use is of a commercial nature or is for nonprofit educational purposes;

(2) the nature of the copyrighted work;

(3) the amount and substantiality of the portion used in relation to the copyrighted work as a whole; and

(4) the effect of the use upon the potential market for or value of the copyrighted work.

Educators should have little or no trouble complying with the "purpose and character of the work" factor. Teachers generally copy materials to aid the educational process. It should be noted, however, that recreational use of copied materials such as videocassettes or computer games is generally not allowed under the statute.

"The nature of the copyrighted work" factor can prove a bit more problematic than "character and purpose of the work." Who determines what is the nature of the work—the creator and/or copyright holder, the teacher, the judge, or the jury? Almost any material can be classified as educational in some context; even a cartoon can be found to have some educational purpose if one is willing to look for it. It seems reasonable that, in determining nature, a court would look to the ordinary use of the work and to the author's intent in creating the work.

The "amount and substantiality" of the work copied is especially troublesome in the use of videocassettes and computer programs. Teachers understand that they are not supposed to copy a whole book, but may not understand that copying a television program or a movie onto videotape or copying a computer program for student use can violate the "amount and substantiality" factor. A relatively new practice, developing libraries of copies, is emerging in some schools. Whether the collections are of print materials or non-print materials, such as videotapes and computer programs, the practice of building collections will generally not be allowed under copyright law.

The last of the four factors, "effect on the market," is also difficult to apply in schools. Arguments can be advanced that students would not rent or purchase commercially available items, even if the copies weren't available. It appears that the use of an author's work without appropriate payment for the privilege is a form of economic harm. Good faith will not operate as an acceptable defense in many copyright cases. In a 1980 New York case, *Roy v. Columbia Broadcasting System*, the court stated: "The federal copyright statute protects copyrighted works against mere copying, even when done in good faith and even when not done to obtain a competitive advantage over the owners of the copyright in the infringed works" (p. 1151).

A Congressional committee developed "Guidelines for Classroom Copying in Not-for-Profit Educational Institutions." Every principal should ensure that teachers have access to copies of the guidelines which are readily available from local libraries, the United States Copyright Office, and members of Congress. Although these guidelines do not have the force of law that the copyright statutes have, judges have used them in deciding cases. Some examples of the guidelines follow.

For poetry, copying of a complete poem of less than 250 words printed on no more than two pages or of an excerpt of 250 words from a longer poem, is allowed. For prose, a complete work of less than 2500 words or an excerpt from a longer work of not more than 1,000 words or 10% of the work, is permitted. The guidelines mandate that copying meet this test of *brevity*.

The copying must be *spontaneous*; the teacher must have decided more or less on the spur of the moment to use an item. Spontaneity presumes that a teacher did not have time to secure permission to use from the copyright holder. A teacher, who decides in September to use certain materials in December, has ample time to seek permission; failure to seek permission in such a situation means that the spontaneity requirement will not be met.

The last requirement is that the copying must not have a *cumulative effect*. Making copies of poems by one author would have a cumulative effect and would mean that collected works of the author would not be bought. Similarly, building video or cassette collections of programs is not permitted. Copying computer programs is never advisable, unless permission to make copies is included in the purchase or rental agreement.

Videotapes may be kept for forty-five days only. During the first ten days, a teacher may use the tape once in a class and once more, if needed, for review. For the remaining thirty-five days teachers may use the tape for evaluative purposes only.

Principals are responsible for compliance with copyright law. If a teacher is charged with copyright violation, it is likely that the principal will be charged as well. Clear policies and careful monitoring of those policies can lessen liability. Copyright violation is stealing. "Thou shalt not steal" is still good law.

A Concluding Thought

The first six decades of this century witnessed few lawsuits against Catholic schools. The situation has changed dramatically in the last twenty years. As the next millennium draws nearer, Catholic educators are becoming increasingly aware of the potential for lawsuits. Study of the law, as it pertains to Catholic schools, is a necessary endeavor for principals and teachers. Efforts to develop and implement policies and procedures that are just to all will help those who serve in the ministry of Catholic education to remain within the requirements of both civil law and the Gospel. Jesus said, "I have come that they may have life and have it more abundantly." Compliance with civil law is one part of the journey to the abundant life that Jesus promised.

GLOSSARY OF TERMS

Board
A board (committee/council/commission) is a body whose members are selected or elected to participate in educational decision-making at the diocesan, regional, inter-parish, or parish level.

Board with Limited Jurisdiction
A board with limited jurisdiction has power limited to certain areas of educational concern. It has final, but not total, jurisdiction in certain areas.

Consultative Board
A consultative board is one which cooperates in the policy-making process by formulating and adapting, but never enacting, policy.

Collegiality
Collegiality is the sharing of responsibility and authority. In the Catholic Church, bishops have the highest authority within a diocese. Powers may be delegated to other parties, such as boards.

Common Law
Common law is that law not created by a legislature. It includes principles of action based on long-established standards of reasonable conduct and on court judgments affirming such standards. It is sometimes called "judge-made law."

Compelling State Interest
A compelling state interest is the serious need for governmental action. The government is said to have a compelling state interest in anti-discrimination legislation or the equal treatment of all citizens.

Contract
A contract is an agreement between two parties. The essentials of a contract are: (1) mutual assent (2) by legally competent parties (3) for consideration (4) to subject matter that is legal and (5) in a form of agreement that is legal.

Consensus
As distinguished from majority rule, consensus is a model of decision-making in which a board seeks to arrive at a decision that all members can agree to support.

Corporal Punishment
Corporal punishment is a type of punishment that involves the infliction of physical pain. Corporal punishment is any touching that can be construed as punitive.

Defamation
Defamation is communication that injures the reputation of another without just cause. Defamation can be either spoken (slander) or written (libel).

Due Process
Due process is fundamental fairness under the law. There are two types:

Substantive Due Process
"The constitutional guarantee that no person shall be arbitrarily deprived of his life, liberty or property; the essence of substantive due process is protection from arbitrary unreasonable action" (Black, p. 1281). Substantive due process involves *what* is done as distinguished from *how* it is done (procedural due process.)

Procedural Due Process
How the process of depriving someone of something is carried out; *how it is done*. The minimum requirements of constitutional due process are *notice* and a *hearing* before an *impartial tribunal*.

Fiduciary
A fiduciary is one who has accepted the responsibility for the care of people or property.

Foreseeability
Foreseeability is "the reasonable anticipation that harm or injury is the likely result of acts or omission" (Black, p. 584). It is not necessary that a person anticipate that a specific injury might result from an action, but only that danger or harm in general might result.

Invasion of Privacy
Invasion of privacy is a tort action in which the plaintiff alleges that the defendant has unreasonably invaded personal privacy, e.g., revealing confidential information in student or personal files without the individual's consent.

Judicial Restraint
Judicial restraint is the doctrine that courts will not interfere in decisions made by professionals.

Landmark Court Decisions
Landmark court decisions are decisions of major importance. These decisions are often used as judicial reasoning in later decisions.

Malpractice
Malpractice is a tort action in which the plaintiff alleges harm resulting from a person's failure to act according to reasonable professional standards.

Negligence
Negligence is the absence of the degree of care which a reasonable person would be expected to use in a given situation.

Policy
A policy is a guide for discretionary action. (CACE/NABE, p. 61). Policy states *what* is to be done, not *how* it is to be done.

Proximate Cause
Proximate cause is a factor contributing to an injury. The injury was a result or reasonably foreseeable outcome of the action or inaction said to be the proximate cause of an injury.

State Action
State action is the presence of the government in an activity to such a degree that the activity may be considered to be that of the government.

Tenure
Tenure is an expectation of continuing employment.

De Facto Tenure:
De facto tenure is an expectation in fact that employment will continue, in the absence of a formal tenure policy. *De facto* tenure can result from past practices of an employer or from length of employment.

Tort
A tort is a civil or private wrong as distinguished from a crime.

BIBLIOGRAPHY

Anthony v. Syracuse University, 231 N.Y.S. 435, 224 App. Div. 487 (1928).

Bischoff v. Brothers of the Sacred Heart, La. App. 416 So. 2d 348 (1982).

Black, Henry Campbell (1979). *Black's law dictionary* (5th ed.) St. Paul: West.

Bloch v. Hillel Torah North Suburban Day School, 438 N.E. 2d 976 (1981).

Board of Education of Long Beach v. Jack M. 566 P. 2d 602 (Cal. 1977).

Bob Jones University v. United States, 103 S. Ct. 2017 (1983).

Board of Regents v. Roth, 408 U.S. 564, 92 S. Ct. 2701 (1972).

Bright v. Isenbarger, 314 F. Supp. 1382 (N.D. Ind. 1970).

Brown v. Tesack, 556 So.2d 84 (La. App. 4th Cir. 1989).

CACE/NABE Governance Task Force (1987). *A Primer on Educational Governance in the Catholic Church.* Washington, D.C.: NCEA.

Clear, Delbert K. and Bagley, Martha (1982). Coaching athletics: a tort just waiting for a judgment? *NOLPE School Law Journal, 10* (2), 184-192.

Canon Law Society (1983). *The code of canon law* (in English translation). London: Collins Liturgical Publications.

Chamelin, Neil C. and Trunzo, Kae B. (1978). Due process and conduct in schools. *Journal of Research and Development in Education*, II, 74-83.

Copyright Act of 1976, U.S.C.A. 101 (1976).

Curry v. Lasell Seminary Co., 1568 Mass. 7 (1897).

Dixon v. Alabama, 186 F. Supp. 945 (1960); reversed at 294 F.2d 150 (U.S.C.A. Fifth Circuit, 1961); cert. den. 368 U.S. 930 (1961).

Dolter v. Wahlert, 483 F.Supp. 266 (N.D. Iowa 1980).

Fee v. Herndon, 900 F.2d 804 (5th Cir. 1990).

Flint v. St. Augustine High School, 323 So.2d 229 (La. App. 1976).
Folan, Patrick M. (1969). Dismissal procedures in private schools. *Harvard Legal Commentary, 6*, pp. 23-30.

Gatti, Richard D. and Gatti, Daniel J. (1983). *New encyclopedic dictionary of school law*. West Nyack, NY: Parker.

Geraci v. St. Xavier High School, 13 Ohio Op. 3d 146 (Ohio, 1978).

Givhan v. Western Line, 439 U.S. 410 (1979).

Goldman, Alvin L. (1966). The university and the liberty of its students—a fiduciary theory. *Kentucky Law Journal, 54*, 643-682.

Goss v. Lopez, 419 U.S. 565 (1975).

Gott v. Berea College, 156 Ky. 376 (1913).

"Guidelines for Off-Air Recording of Broadcast Programming for Educational Purposes." *CONG. REC.* E4750 (daily edition October 14, 1981).

Hall v. Tawney, 621 F.2d 607 (1980).

Holy Names School v. Retlick, 326 N.W.2d 121 (Wis. App. 1983).

Horton, J.L. and Corcoran, V. (1985). *Pre-employment inquiries.* Topeka: National Organization on Legal Problems of Education.

Illinois v. Burdette Wehmeyer, 509 N.E.2d 605 (1987).

Ingraham v. Wright, 430 U.S. 65 (1977).

Keyishian v. Board of Regents, 385 U.S. 589 (1967).

LaMorte, Michael W. (1977). Rights and responsibilities in the light of social contract theory. *Educational Administration Quarterly, 13,* pp. 31-48.

Levandoski v. Jackson, 328 So.2d 339 (Minn. 1976).

Little v. St. Mary Magdalene Parish, 739 F.Supp. 1003 (1990).

Marcus v. Rowley, 695 F.2d 1171 (9th Cir. 1983).

Mt. Healthy v. Doyle, 429 U.S. 274 (1977).

NLRB v. Catholic Bishop of Chicago, 440 U.S. 490 (1979).

New Jersey v. T.L.O., 105 S. Ct. 733 (1985).

O'Brien, Francis W. (1974). Due process for the non-tenured in private schools. *Journal of Law and Education, 3,* 175-202.

Perry v. Sindermann, 408 U.S. 593 (1972).

Pierce v. the Society of Sisters, 268 U.S. 510 (1925).

Pickering v. B.O.E., 391 U.S. 563 (1968).

Reardon v. LeMoyne, 454 A.2d 428 (N.H. 1982).

Rendell-Baker v. Kohn, 102 S. Ct. 2764 (1982).

Reutter, E.E., Jr. (1981). *Schools and the law.* Reston, Virginia: NASSP.

Roy v. Columbia Broadcasting, 503 F.Supp. 1137 (S.D.N.Y. 1979).

Seavey, Warren A. (1957). Dismissal of students: due process. *Harvard Law Review, 70*, 1406-1410.

Segerman v. Jones, 259 A.2d (Maryland, 1969).

Shaughnessy, Mary Angela (1991). *Extended care programs in Catholic schools: some legal concerns.* Washington, D.C.: NCEA.

Shaughnessy, Mary Angela (1988). *A primer on school law: a guide for board members in Catholic schools.* Washington, D.C.: NCEA.

Shaughnessy, Mary Angela (1989). *School handbooks: some legal considerations.* Washington, D.C.: NCEA, 1988.

Sheehan v. St. Peter's Catholic High School, 188 N.W. 2d 868 (Minn. 1971).

Smith v. Archbishop of St. Louis, 632 S.W.2d 516 (Mo. Ct. App. 1982).

Station v. Travelers Insurance Co., 292 So. 2d 289 (La. Ct. App. 1974).

Steeber v. Benilde-St. Margaret's High School, (No. D.C. 739 378, Hennepin County, Minn., 1978).

Thrasher v. General Casualty Co. of Wisconsin, 732 F. Supp. 966 (W.D. Wisc. 1990).

Tinker v. Des Moines Independent School District, 393 U.S. 503 (1969).

Titus v. Lindberg, 228 A.2d 65 (New Jersey, 1967).

20 United States Code, Sec. 1232g, The Buckley Amendment, Family Education Rights and Privacy Act (1974).

United States Code Annotated.

Valente, William D. (1980). *Law in the Schools*. Columbus: Merrill.

Weithoff v. St. Veronica School, 210 N.W.2d 108 (Mich. 1973).

Wisch v. Sanford School, 420 F. Supp. 1310 (D. Del. 1976).

Wood v. Strickland, 420 U.S. 308 (1974).

INDEX

Mary Angela Shaughnessy

Sister Mary Angela Shaughnessy is a Sister of Charity of Nazareth who has taught at all levels of Catholic education from elementary through graduate school. She served eight years as principal of a Catholic school. She holds a bachelor's degree in English and a master's degree in education from Spalding University, a master's degree in English from the University of Louisville, and a Ph.D. in educational administration and supervision from Boston University. A regular speaker at NCEA conventions, she has presented numerous workshops and lectures on Catholic schools and the law across the country. She is an adjunct professor in Boston College's Catholic School Leadership Program in and the University of San Francisco's Institute for Catholic Educational Leadership. Currently, Sister Mary Angela is Associate Professor of Education and Director of Doctoral Studies in Education at Spalding University, Louisville, Kentucky. She is the author of three NCEA texts: the 1988 *A Primer on School Law: A Guide for Board Members in Catholic Schools*, the 1989 *School Handbooks: Some Legal Considerations*, and the 1990 *Extended Care Programs in Catholic Schools: Some Legal Concerns*. She is also the author of *Catholic Schools and the Law: A Teacher's Guide* published in 1990 by the Paulist Press.